Nicos Poulantzas

London: NLB

Atlantic Highlands: HUMANITIES PRESS

The Crisis
of the Dictatorships

Portugal

Greece

Spain

Translated by David Fernbach

Library of Congress Cataloging in Publication Data

Poulantzas, Nicos Ar
   The crisis of the dictatorships.
   Translation of La crise des dictatures.
   Includes index.
1. Portugal—Politics and government—1933-1974.
2. Greece, Modern—Politics and government—1967-
3. Spain—Politics and government—1939-1975.   1. Title.
DP680.P6613   320.9′469′042   76-27303

First published as *La Crise des Dictatures*
by François Maspero, 1975
© François Maspero, 1975

This edition first published 1976

© NLB, 1976

Filmset by Servis Filmsetting Ltd, Manchester
Printed and bound in Great Britain by
Marston Book Services Ltd, Oxfordshire

NLB, 7 Carlisle Street, London W1
ISBN 902308 77 7

Contents

Preface

The past two years in Europe have witnessed a series of events of considerable significance: the overthrow of the military dictatorships in Portugal and Greece; and the accelerated decay of the Franco régime in Spain, so that its overthrow is now also on the historical agenda.

Both the path taken by the fall of the Portuguese and Greek dictatorships, and the process now under way in Spain, raise a number of important questions which are still far from being resolved. The basic pivot in these is as follows. The Portuguese and Greek regimes were evidently not overthrown by an open and frontal movement of the popular masses in insurrection, nor by a foreign military intervention, as was the case with Italian fascism and Nazism in Germany. What then are the factors that determined their overthrow, and what form has the intervention of the popular masses taken in this conjuncture?

These are not just questions bearing only on Portugal, Greece and Spain. They also concern, in particular, several other countries which have in common with those we are dealing with here that they stand in a relationship of dependence to the imperialist metropolises and are similarly marked by exceptional capitalist regimes (fascism, bonapartism, military dictatorship); we need only note the numerous examples in Latin America. The lessons that may be drawn from the European dictatorships are of major importance in this respect.

But some of these questions also concern the 'industrialized' and 'free' countries of Europe, as they are called. For Greece, Portugal and Spain are characterized by a special kind of dependence. These countries are no longer marked by the condition referred to descriptively as 'under-development'. As far as their economic and social structure is concerned, they are firmly in the European arena. The events taking place there are thus directly relevant, at least in some respects, to the other European countries.

These then are the questions that this essay deals with, and to which it sets out to give at least a preliminary rough answer. With this in mind, I must make the following points here, for the sake of clarification.

1) My intention has been to produce a short text of political theory, limited to the basic questions; it is in no way exhaustive, and does not present a detailed history of these regimes and their overthrow. It is addressed to a relatively well-informed readership, who have been following the events in these countries with a political interest, and can thus to a certain extent dispense with a factual description and concentrate on underlying causes and their explanation. Nevertheless, and so as not to make the presentation too dry, I have brought in what seemed to me the most important concrete material, in an effort to avoid the usual danger of this type of analysis, i.e. to say at the same time too much and too little.

2) The overthrow of the Portuguese and Greek regimes, and the process elapsing in Spain, seem to me to exhibit certain common features, at least as far as the basic factors involved are concerned. This is frequently despite manifest appearances, and the reasons for this I shall explain. While I have also been concerned to point out the important differences that remain, I have sought above all to keep in mind these similarities, even though this obviously involves a certain degree of schematism.

3) There is one major absence in this text which is entirely deliberate. Even though I frequently indicate the role that

organizations of the left have played in these processes, I have not gone into their actions in any detail, confining myself to bringing out what is to a certain extent the effect of these actions, namely the particular role of the popular masses. This is in no way because I under-estimate the action of these organizations, but for quite the opposite reason. In order to deal properly with their role, it would have been necessary to embark on an exhaustive discussion of political strategies and the questions of political theory that underlie them, and this would have involved a separate book. Faced here in particular with the danger of saying both too much and too little, I have made the definite choice of leaving the ground untrodden for the time being.

4) This essay, therefore, is not envisaged as anything more than a contribution to the discussion already under way on the events that have taken place up till now, particularly with respect to the process of democratization, and the lessons to be drawn from them. Above all, it does not claim to define the paths that these countries will follow in the future, and this is particularly true for Portugal, given the instability of the present balance of forces in that country.

5) One final remark – in certain analyses and positions taken in this text, the reader will find some departures from my book *Fascism and Dictatorship*, published originally in 1970. To some extent these differences bear on the different nature of the object under consideration, in the present case regimes of military dictatorship which are not in the strict sense fascist, and which are located in a different historical period from that of the inter-war years. But these differences are also due in part to certain rectifications of my previous analyses, due to the fact that events in these countries have undeniably presented a series of new elements in the experience of popular movements confronting the exceptional capitalist regimes (regimes of open war against the popular masses).

Paris, February 1975

I

The Imperialist World Context

The events that have taken place in Portugal and Greece, and the process now beginning in Spain, can only be properly grasped in terms of the new world context in which they are located: in other words, the new phase of imperialism, and its effects on the European countries. Within the European arena, Portugal, Greece and Spain in fact exhibit, if in different degrees, a characteristic type of dependence in relation to the imperialist metropolises, and to the United States as their dominant centre.

It would be wrong to foist on these countries the traditional notion of 'under-development'. By their economic and social structure, they are now part of Europe; their proximity is not only geographic, nor even predominantly so. Anticipating somewhat, we can even say that certain features of the new dependence that they present in relation to the United States and to the other European countries (the EEC) also character-ize, in this new phase of imperialism, those European countries that themselves form part of the imperialist metropolises, in their own relationship to the United States. That does not mean that Portugal, Spain and Greece do not have a particular form of dependence; this is indeed a specific feature of the events that have taken place there.

This specific form of dependence, which is a function of the particular history of these countries, has two aspects to it:

– on the one hand, the aspect of an old-established primitive accumulation of capital, deriving in the Portuguese and Spanish cases from the exploitation of their colonies, and in

the Greek case from exploitation of the Eastern Mediterranean, which distinguishes these countries from the particular type of dependence of other dominated countries;
  – on the other hand, the blockage, due to several reasons, of
an endogenous accumulation of capital at the right time,
which puts them right alongside other countries dependent
on the imperialist metropolises in the present phase of
imperialism; the new structure of dependence specific to this
phase is thus of the highest importance.

The principal characteristic in this respect is therefore the
present phase of imperialism. Since the beginnings of
imperialism, the relationships between national social formations (metropolitan countries/dominated and dependent
countries) have been marked by the primacy of the export of
capital over the export of commodities. Yet this definition is
still too general; in actual fact, the export of capital plays a
variable role, according to the phases of imperialist development, and this can only be understood in relation to the
transformations of production relations and labour processes
on the world scale.

During earlier phases, in fact, export of capital from the
imperialist countries to the dependent countries was chiefly
bound up with the control of raw materials (extractive
industries) and the extension of markets. In conjunction with
this, the principal dividing line between the metropolitan
countries and the dominated and dependent ones was still
essentially that between industry and agriculture, or between
town and country. Thus the capitalist mode of production
that was dominant in its monopoly form in the imperialist
metropolises and the imperialist chain as a whole, had not yet
succeeded in incorporating and dominating the relations of
production within the dependent countries themselves.
Inside these countries, other modes and forms of production
(the feudal mode of production, and the form of petty
commodity production) displayed a remarkable persistence,
even though suitably transformed by the penetration of
capitalist relationships.

This situation had substantial effects on the socio-economic structure of the countries involved, and even on their political structure: the preponderant and highly characteristic role of agriculture and the extraction of raw materials, combined with a marked delay in the process of industrialization, which has often been seen in terms of the incorrect notion of 'under-development'. The consequence of this, on the side of the dominated classes, was: a) the numerical weakness and relatively slight social and political weight of the working class, in relation to the substantial weight of a peasantry still subordinated to precapitalist relations of production; b) the quite particular disposition of the petty bourgeoisie, within which could be distinguished an important traditional petty bourgeoisie in manufacture, handicrafts (small-scale production) and commerce, and the substantial weight of a state petty bourgeoisie (agents of the state apparatus) due to the parasitic growth of the state bureaucracy characteristic of this dependent situation. On the side of the dominant classes, this situation was manifested in a particular configuration of the power bloc, often denoted by the term 'oligarchy': big landed proprietors, whose weight was very substantial, allied to a characteristically comprador big bourgeoisie, whose own economic base in the country was weak, and who functioned chiefly as a commercial and financial intermediary for the penetration of foreign imperialist capital, being closely controlled by this foreign capital.

The present phase of imperialism has seen major changes; the beginnings of these may be located in the immediate post-war years, though their consolidation and expanded reproduction began only in the 1960s. Capital export still serves for the control of raw materials and the extension of markets, but this is no longer its principal function. The principal function of the export of capital today essentially derives from the need for imperialist monopoly capital to valorize itself on the world scale by turning to profit every relative advantage in the direct exploitation of labour. What is involved here is a characteristic feature of the falling rate of profit tendency, and the new conditions in which an average rate of profit is established in the present world context.

The drive to counter-act this tendency runs principally by way of the intensive exploitation of labour on a world scale (increase in the rate of exploitation in the form of relative surplus-value, by raising labour productivity, technological innovations, etc.). This involves the reproduction of capitalist relations of production actually within the dependent countries themselves, where these relations subordinate labour-power on an increasing scale, and it corresponds to both a prodigious socialization of labour processes and to a marked internationalization of capital on the world scale.

These changes have important implications for the dependent countries, or at least for certain of their number; the foreign capital invested in them increasingly takes the form of direct investment in the sector of productive industrial capital. The share of this foreign capital that is invested in manufacturing industry is growing rapidly. The case that has attracted most attention here is that of the great multi-national corporations, though this is only a limited index of the phenomenon. These multinationals are for the most part American, and in certain of the dependent countries they produce substantial portions of the finished products that they sell on the world market, because of the favourable costs of production there; alternatively they establish an entire stage of their overall production in dependent countries, or else assemble there finished products for local sale. This phenomenon, however, goes far beyond the particular case of the multinational corporations; the point is that the direction of foreign capital investments in these countries involves their labour processes in the capitalist socialization of these processes on the world scale.

This new organization of the imperialist chain and its associated dependence, of which Greece and Spain are typical examples and Portugal only somewhat less so, substantially alters the internal socio-economic structure of the countries subjected to it. Their position as dominated and dependent countries no longer means simply a traditional division between them and the imperialist metropolises along the lines industry/agriculture; this dependence now precisely involves their industrialization under the aegis of foreign capital and at its instigation. Capitalist relations of production are reproduced on a massive scale within these countries themselves, subordinating labour-power while distorting, reorganizing and even hastening the dissolution of pre-capitalist relationships.

It follows, therefore, that Spain and Greece have not ceased to be dominated and dependent countries, with Portugal following in their wake, because they have emerged from some so-called state of 'under-development' – contrary to what is maintained by the entire 'development' ideology. In their case, the domination and dependence that foreign imperialist capital inflicts on them are simply taking, on the whole, a new turn. It now involves the actual process of productive industrial capital and the labour processes that pertain to it at the international level. This is in fact the phenomenon of *dependent industrialization*, which is also displayed by certain other dependent countries, particularly in Latin America, and exhibits the following features:

(i) These countries are confined to forms of industry based on low-level technology.

(ii) Labour productivity is kept at a low level, controlled by the integration of the labour processes in these countries into a socialization of the productive forces (integrated production) which, in the bipolar tendency of qualification/disqualification of labour-power that is characteristic of monopoly capital, exports the disqualification aspect to the dominated countries, while reserving the reproduction of highly skilled labour for the dominant countries.

(iii) The profits directly realized from the production of surplus-value by labour-power in the dominated countries are to a high degree expatriated.

To the exploitation of the popular masses by the productive investment of foreign capital is added a supplementary element, in this case involving the actual labour-power of these countries in the new internationalization of capitalist relations as a whole: the export of labour-power to the imperialist metropolises – the migrant workers – which Portugal, Greece and Spain provide for Europe on a grand scale. This haemorrhage of these countries' labour-power constitutes a real superexploitation of the popular masses by the dominant imperialist capital, not just in the superexploitation that these workers suffer in the 'host' countries, but also, and even more, in the training costs that the dominated countries lose for labour-power that bears fruit in the dominant countries. Furthermore, and we shall come back to this later, this massive emigration is precisely rendered possible by the process of distorted industrialization that foreign capital promotes in these countries, and by the internal dislocations and de-centerings provoked by this induced reproduction of the dominant capitalist relationships.

This new organization of exploitation and dependence in the imperialist chain thus gives rise to new cleavages between the dominated and dependent countries themselves. While certain of them continue to experience, as the dominant form of their exploitation by foreign capital, an export of capital bound up with the control of raw material and the export of commodities, and with a division between industry and agriculture, the form of exploitation that is dominant in our case, though in parallel with old forms only gradually on the retreat, follows a new course.[1]

While I do not want to tire the reader with detailed figures, I shall just give a few examples here, in order to illustrate and situate the socio-economic structure of the countries we are concerned with, and their evolution in the course of recent years.

In *Portugal*, though the policy of economic development based on development plans dates from 1953, it was only from 1960 that the penetration of foreign capital in substantial amounts began to quicken, in conjunction with a parallel process of industrial expansion. The volume of direct

---

[1] I have dealt with this question, as with several others that will appear later on, such as the present relations between the United States and Europe, the domestic bourgeoisie, etc., in *Classes in Contemporary Capitalism*, NLB, 1975.

foreign investment doubled between 1963 and 1965, and it has continued to grow ever since. Foreign investment has been more and more concentrated in the different sectors of productive industrial capital, through subsidiary branches of the multinationals (chemical, engineering and electronics industries, as well as various other manufacturing industries such as clothing). Parallel with this, the Portuguese GNP has increased by around 6 per cent per year since 1960; what is more, this breaks down, between 1960 and 1970, into a growth rate of 9.1 per cent in industry, 1.5 per cent in agriculture, and 5.9 per cent in the service sector. In 1971, the primary sector only employed 31.8 per cent of the active population (as against 48.4 per cent in 1950), industry 37.2 per cent (24.9 per cent in 1950) and services 32 per cent (26.7 per cent in 1950). The special characteristic of Portuguese capitalism, moreover, compared with that of Greece and Spain, is the extreme concentration and centralization of capital, particularly given the level of industrialization: 168 companies out of a total of 40,000 (i.e. 0.4 per cent) hold at least 53 per cent of the total capital.

In *Spain*, although the first burst of industrialization also dates from 1953, following the economic and political agreements concluded with the United States, which opened Spain up to the penetration of American capital, the process only began to accelerate towards the end of the so-called 'stabilization' period, i.e. round about 1960. Since then, foreign investment has increased quite spectacularly (from 36.1 million dollars in 1960 to around 180 million in 1968); here, too, it is concentrated, through branches of the multinationals, in the chemical industry, electrical equipment and heavy engineering (shipbuilding, automobiles), and various other manufacturing industries. The rate of increase in the Spanish GNP reached an annual average of around 7 per cent in the 1960s, due chiefly to the expansion of industrial production, which increased four times between 1956 and 1969. By 1969, the agricultural sector only employed 31 per cent of the active population (against 42 per cent in 1960), industry 36 per cent (32 per cent in 1960), and services 33 per cent (27 per cent in 1960).

In *Greece*, the process is all the more interesting in so far as it is possible to compare development from 1960 under a democratic regime, with that from 1967 onwards under the military dictatorship. Here, too, the process of industrialization got under way at the beginning of the 1960s, together with the penetration of foreign capital. The volume of foreign investment increased five times between 1960 and 1964; 1965 and 1966, moreover, were marked by an exceptional and spectacular advance in foreign capital due to the massive investments of Esso-Pappas and Pechiney in these two years. Between 1960 and 1967, the Greek GNP grew at an annual average of 6.7 per cent.

Under the military regime – according to the official figures – the influx of foreign capital into Greece increased by 62 per cent, comparing the years 1967–71 with 1962–66. Moreover, certain other investments that the regime anticipated and bent itself to secure did not ultimately come to fruition, some foreign investors showing hesitation in view of the regime's 'instability'.) The rate of increase in the GNP under the military dictatorship was as follows:

	per cent
1967:	4.5
1968:	5.8
1969:	8.8
1970:	7.5
1971:	7.3
1972:	10.5
1973:	10.1

Here again, foreign investment was concentrated from 1960 onwards in the sector of productive industrial capital (chemicals, electrical engineering, shipbuilding, other manufacturing industry). Between 1960 and 1970, Greek subsidiaries of the multinationals accounted for 45 per cent of the increase in industrial production. The most striking rate of increase, throughout this whole period, is that shown by manufacturing industry: some 10.3 per cent per year between

1963 and 1970. The percentage of the active population employed in agriculture fell from 56 per cent in 1961 to 45 per cent in 1967, and to 37.3 per cent in 1971; that in industry rose from 14 per cent in 1961 to 21.2 per cent in 1967, and reached 25 per cent in 1971 (in which year services employed 38 per cent). We may note that this distribution of the active population in Greece does not fully register the industrialization of the country, which is shown more clearly by the fact that agriculture only accounted for 18 per cent of the GNP in 1970, while industry made up 33.2 per cent; this is because industrialization here has been intensive, through the increase in labour productivity in certain sectors (chemicals, petroleum products, shipbuilding).

The new form of dependence, which goes together with a particular type of industrialization, is also shown by a whole series of other particular features: the growing volume of manufactured products in these countries' exports, for example, relative to agricultural exports. But the decisive significance of this new path of dependence lies above all in the modifications that it brings about in socio-economic structures.

We are already faced with a problem here: this state of affairs has often been under-estimated by the resistance organizations. This was particularly the case in Portugal, traditionally seen as a 'backward' country, but also in Spain, where the resistance organizations took a long time to recognize these new realities. The underlying reason is the tradition bequeathed by the Third International, which considered fascist regimes and military dictatorships as necessarily bound up with economic retardment or retrogression; there are a host of formulations according to which these regimes are supposed to have caused a long-term 'blockage' of these countries' 'economic development', or even put it into reverse. These characterizations go hand in hand with an economist/technicist conception of economic development and industrialization, a conception that pervades the various theories of underdevelopment, itself a highly erroneous term. For there is no such thing as a neutral economic development, economic development as such, with a uniform and unambiguous direction that could only be positive: an economic development which cannot be properly carried out by these regimes, so that condemning them necessarily involves characterizing them as 'economically retrogressive'. Here a further and related illusion comes to light: these regimes are seen as condemned inevitably to disappear, and their fall directly predicated on their supposed inability to set under way, or follow through, 'economic development'.

But this 'development as such' lacks any meaning. What matters is its social and political significance, i.e. its relationship to the exploitation of the popular masses in the contemporary imperialist chain. And roughly since the 1960s, if not always to the same extent, the Portuguese and Spanish regimes have followed, and the Greek military regime continued, a policy of industrial development parallel with a concentration and centralization of capital; in other words, a policy of development of capitalist relations in their monopoly form, and one conforming with the new features of exploitation that mark the present phase of imperialism and the relationships between dominant and dominated countries – a policy, therefore, that by this very fact subjugates these countries to the new dependence that characterizes the imperialist chain. One outcome of this is that this 'economic development' exhibits a series of aspects specific to the dependent industrialization of the dominated countries, an industrialization that is very far from following the path of the dominant countries; another outcome is that the popular masses have experienced a considerably increased exploitation both by their own dominant classes and by those of the imperialist metropolises, from the very fact of this industrialization.

This already sheds light on the question of the relation between the dictatorships and the type of dependence and development peculiar to these countries. It is an undeniable fact that these regimes have particularly favoured this path of dependence on foreign imperialist capital. We have had to make this point already at this stage of the argument, as a number of writers, partly in reaction to the erroneous thesis that the dictatorships are associated with an 'economic retardment', accept that these regimes have promoted the development of capitalism, but immediately add, as if afraid of having conceded a point, that this makes no difference, as the same development would have taken place anyway, and in the same manner, if these countries had had bourgeois-democratic regimes. Greece is generally given as the example here, as the hypothesis cannot be verified in the cases of Spain and Portugal, where the dictatorships were established so long ago. Greece saw the beginnings of industrialization marked by the new structures of dependence and the massive investment of foreign capital, before the dictatorship, a process that was moreover accelerated from 1964 onwards, under not a right-wing government, but rather one of the centre (George Papandreou). The junta, then, can simply be said to have continued on the course already established. In this conception, the place of a country in the imperialist chain is seen as sufficient to determine the forms of its dependence in all their details: socio-political distinctions and the internal political institutions of the country would be unable to alter this, except in the case of a transition to socialism.

But we must be clear as to what is involved here. It is obvious that a country's dependence vis-à-vis imperialism can only be broken by a process of national liberation, which in the new phase of imperialism and the present circumstances as a whole, coincides with a process of transition to socialism. This accepted, however, there are certainly different forms and degrees of dependence, and these essentially depend on the specific internal socio-political coordinates of the countries involved. To take a simple example, the relation of France to American capital was evidently different under the Gaullism of the years 1960–68 than it has been since – today above all – and yet these two moments are both located in the same, present phase of imperialism. In this sense, the dictatorial regimes in Portugal, Spain and Greece certainly played an important role in the specific pattern, shape and rhythm of the dependence process that took place under their direction; not because of their inherent differences from the parliamentary-democratic form of regime, but rather because of the economic and social forces whose interests they predominantly represented. This was particularly the case in Greece, where the military dictatorship's policy in this respect was very different from that of the previous regime. To formulate the problem more clearly: the specific forms of regime in the dependent countries play a particular role in the precise forms assumed there by the new path of dependence, as a result of the specific 'internal' balance of forces to which they correspond.

One basic strand in the present analysis has now been already indicated.

In examining forms of regime and the changes in political institutions, a problem which arises for the imperialist metropolises as well as for the dependent countries, it is essential to take the present phase of capitalism into consideration. This phase, however, does not simply determine all these forms and changes by itself; it is only relevant in so far as it determines, the conjunctures of class struggle, the transformations of classes and the internal balances of socio-political forces which alone can explain these regimes and their evolution. To put it another way, we can certainly speak at a general and rather abstract level of a *dependent type of state*, for the dependent societies of the present time: a state that exhibits certain common features in all the societies in which it occurs, in so far as it corresponds to the general modifications that imperialism inflicts on them, and must fulfil the general functions falling to it in the present phase of imperialism. But it is none the less clear that the concrete forms that this state assumes – fascism, military dictatorship, 'democratic' republic, etc. – depend on internal factors within these societies. These factors appear as decisive as soon as one accepts that it makes a considerable difference, at least for these countries themselves and the popular masses there, whether this dependent state is a bourgeois 'democracy' or a reactionary military dictatorship; here, as elsewhere, the forms that bourgeois domination assumes are far from a matter of indifference, for all their common appellation as 'dictatorships of the bourgeoisie'.

Maintaining the primacy of internal factors in this way already takes us a step further; we have to break once and for all with a mechanistic and almost topological (if not 'geographical') conception of the relation between internal and external factors. In the present phase of imperialism there is really no such thing as external factors on the one hand, acting purely from 'outside', and opposed to internal factors 'isolated' in their own 'space' and outclassing the others. If we maintain the primacy of internal factors, we simply mean that those coordinates of the imperialist chain that are 'external' to a country – the global balance of forces, the role of a particular great power, etc. – only act on the country in question by way of their internalization, i.e. by their articulation to its own specific contradictions. But these contradictions themselves, in certain aspects, represent the induced reproduction of the contradictions of the imperialist chain within the various individual countries. To talk of internal factors in this sense, then, is to discover the real role that imperialism (uneven development) plays in the evolution of the various social formations.

This will be the guiding thread in the following analyses, and its implications involve a whole series of problems. To make this more clear, we can turn for a moment to the case of Chile, which is highly relevant as regards the role of the imperialist powers – and their centre in particular, the United States – in the installation, maintenance and evolution of the regimes we are concerned with here. In discussions of the Chilean experience the mechanistic and topological conception of 'external factors' is often at work in the thesis of the *plot* against the Allende government, a thesis which maintains the supposedly direct, immediate and exhaustive role played by the United States and the CIA. This thesis has the particular advantage that it prevents the Allende government's own errors from being examined, and above all, closes people's eyes to those internal conjunctures which are precisely what enabled 'outside intervention' and the 'hand of the foreigner' to be effective. No one can doubt today that there have been and continue to be such interventions. But except in the extreme case of open and direct intervention on a massive scale (Santo Domingo, Vietnam, etc.), this cannot generally play a decisive role in the dependent countries concerned — particularly in such European countries as Portugal, Greece and Spain — without being articulated, within these countries, to the internal balance of forces.

II

The Dictatorships, the United States and Europe

Before coming to the internal causes of the decomposition (Spain) and fall (Portugal, Greece) of these regimes, we must first examine the world conjuncture of imperialism as it concretely affects these countries.

To start with the economic level. I have already noted that the Portuguese, Spanish and Greek regimes systematically promoted the investment of foreign imperialist capital. This capital is invested in the countries concerned both to directly exploit the popular masses there, and to use these countries as a staging-post in the exploitation of other countries. In Portugal in particular, not only did the dictatorship directly promote the pillage of its African colonies by foreign capital, but the part of this capital invested in Portugal itself was also largely oriented toward the colonies. Greece was also used by foreign capital as a base for the conquest of African markets, and for re-export of capital to African countries under the 'neutral' Greek label.

Let us pause for a moment on the policies of promoting foreign investment that were pursued by these countries. We can certainly note that similar policies were also pursued by the governments of several other European countries (Germany, Great Britain, etc.) vis-à-vis American capital. In the cases we are dealing with here, however, this took particular forms. The facilities granted (tax exemptions, almost unlimited opportunity of repatriating profits, capital grants, monopoly privileges, leonine contracts with national firms), the absence of any real control, and so on, are without any parallel in the other European countries. This is particularly striking in Greece, where the situation can be compared with the policy of the governments that preceded the military junta, such as that of Karamanlis (conservative), which also promoted the penetration of foreign capital. As regards the facilities granted to foreign capital for an unbridled pillage of the country, the junta's policy towards foreign capital was qualitatively different from that of the previous governments. (This was particularly the case with foreign capital in Greek shipping.)

It should be understood, of course, that the facilities in question are not just those explicitly granted. It is easy to see how foreign capital can also profit from the internal situation in a country and the repression that weighs upon the working class and the popular masses (abolition of the right to strike, the ban on working-class organization, etc.).

These points are sufficiently well-known not to need particular emphasis here. But what is important to stress, as it directly locates these countries at the very heart of present inter-imperialist contradictions, is the gradual increase in the economic relations tying these nations to the European Common Market, as opposed to those tying them to the United States.

This is particularly apparent at the level of foreign capital investment.

In Portugal, for instance, capital from the EEC countries is massively dominant, in particular capital from West Germany and the United Kingdom. In 1971 the respective shares of new foreign investment, in millions of escudos, were: United States 391.6; West Germany 237.1; United Kingdom 156.2; France 72.6. In 1972, United States 300.3; West Germany 589.0; United Kingdom 298.6; France 74.7. In 1973, United States 238.9; West Germany 815.4; United Kingdom 552.3; France 109.6.

In Spain, the percentage of American capital in the total volume of foreign investment followed an upward curve from 1961 to around 1965, rising from 27.8 per cent to 48.3 per cent of the total, but it has since progressively fallen, to a level of 29.2 per cent in 1970.

In Greece, although American investment remains massively predominant, there has also been a spectacular increase in investment from the EEC, particularly from France, which now holds second place.

The same situation is to be seen in the field of foreign trade: trade with the Common Market as a proportion of total foreign trade has increased spectacularly in the cases of Portugal and Greece, and somewhat less strikingly in the case of Spain, in relation to trade with the United States.

This all leads to a most important question. Did the present contradictions between the United States and the European Common Market play a role in the decline and fall of the dictatorships, and if so, what exactly? What in particular has been the role of the special relationships that these countries have had with the Common Market, a relationship that in the case of Greece was already institutionalized, but officially frozen during the colonels' regime, while a similarly institutionalized relationship was also sought systematically by Portugal under Caetano and is still sought by the present Spanish government?

To situate the role played here by the inter-imperialist contradictions between the United States and Europe, we must first establish their general significance at the present time. The development and extension of the Common Market, combined with the dollar crisis, led several writers to foresee the inevitable demise of American hegemony, with Europe coming to form an effective 'counter-imperialism' to the United States. We may note in passing that these are often the same writers who indulged in the myth of 'ultra-imperialism' during the long period in which inter-imperialist contradictions seemed relatively quiescent – the myth of an uncontested hegemony and domination by the United States over the entire imperialist world, which it had allegedly succeeded in pacifying under its own aegis.

Both these notions are equally false. If American hegemony is now in retreat, in relation to certain quite exceptional characteristics that it assumed when the European economies had suffered partial destruction as a result of the Second

World War, it is still the case that the extension and development of the Common Market has gone together with a prodigious growth in direct American investment, more and more involving sectors of directly productive capital (manufacturing industries) in the EEC countries. The privileged location of American foreign investment is no longer the Third World, but precisely the European Common Market: the case of West Germany, now the dominant economy within the Common Market, is highly significant here, to say nothing of Great Britain. This actually creates a new form of dependence of the European countries on the United States, and a quite particular form, as it cannot be identified with that affecting the dominated countries in their relationship with the imperialist metropolises as a whole, being in no way analogous to this. It can only be understood in terms of an internationalization of capital and of capitalist relations, not in terms of competing 'national economies'. The confirmation of this new dependence can be found in the way that the Common Market has successively capitulated to the United States, on many questions, in the present crisis period, and particularly the way that its members have operated and capitulated individually in the face of American demands (over monetary policy, energy, etc.). One effect of this new dependence is the absence of any real unification of capital at the present time between the various European countries. Relations between them have in fact an external centre, passing by way of the relationship that each of these countries maintains individually with the United States. This factor is important to bear in mind with regard to the EEC's attitude to the dictatorships.

Secondly, however, there is a real reactivation and intensification of inter-imperialist contradictions, correlative with the present crisis of capitalism, between the United States and the European Common Market, and one that is in no way incompatible with what has just been said. It is only the notion of 'ultraimperialism' that identifies the hegemony of one imperialist country over others with a complete 'pacification' of inter-imperialist contradictions, so that the reactivation of these contradictions is immediately seen as the elimination of this hegemony. At the present moment, these contradictions are becoming more intense; battles are taking place for the conquest of protected territories, both for capital export, to counteract the tendential fall in the rate of profit (recession) in the imperialist centres, and also for the export of commodities and the control of raw materials, in the context of the imbalances in international payments that have marked the past few years. There are also intense struggles for control of countries that can serve as intermediate staging-posts for imperialist capital in its further expansion: the characteristic cases of Portugal and Greece. The problem of oil has simply accentuated this state of affairs.

As far as the countries we are concerned with here are concerned, the contradictions between the United States and the Common Market are expressed particularly by way of the independent strategy that the Common Market is pursuing in the Mediterranean region. The question remains, however, as to what role these contradictions played in the overthrow or changes in the Portuguese, Greek and Spanish regimes.

Taking up the points already made, I maintain, firstly, that these contradictions did not play any direct or immediate role, and secondly, that it would be quite wrong to believe that the EEC consistently played the democratic card, as it were, in order to challenge American interests which were exclusively represented by these dictatorships. The contradiction between the United States and Europe is not in fact an explosive contradiction between two equivalent counter-imperialisms (Europe as a 'third force'), contending for hegemony step by step; it is essentially a contradiction centring on a rearrangement in the balance of forces, but still always under American hegemony. The dictatorships themselves, moreover, and this applies to Caetano, Papadopoulos/Markezinis and to the Opus Dei episode under Franco, explicitly sought integration into the Common Market, the reason for this being, as we shall see, the complex relationships that they maintained with the various fractions of their own bourgeoisies. Even though these attempts proved unsuccessful, it was precisely under these regimes that the import of European capital into these countries and the volume of trade on preferential terms between them and Europe grew to significant proportions, in some respects supplanting economic relations with the United States.

Nothing would be more wrong, then, than to view the Common Market as having in any way subjected these regimes to an economic boycott. For all the declarations on the European side, justifying refusal of EEC membership on the grounds of the absence of democratic institutions, the real reason why these countries have not been integrated into the Common Market is related to the very real problems of European agricultural policy, which would be directly threatened by these countries acquiring full membership status, and the effect this would have on their agricultural exports to the EEC. This is shown by the difficulties still encountered today as regards the integration into the Common Market of Greece and Portugal. The EEC's economic strategy towards these countries did not simply hinge on a change in their regimes, and this can only be understood if the notion of an explosive and antagonistic contradiction between the United States and the Common Market is abandoned.

This does not mean that this contradiction did not play an important role in the decline and fall of the dictatorships; simply that its role is expressed in a very particular way.

1. It is basically expressed in the induced and specific reproduction of this contradiction actually within these countries, and principally by the effects that this contradiction has on the internal differentiation of their dominant classes (we will deal with this more fully in the following chapter). The contradiction United States/Europe, which is structured into the present process of internationalization of capital, is directly reflected in various internal divisions and strategic differentiations of the endogenous capital in these countries, according to the divergent lines of dependence that polarize it either towards American capital or towards European. It should also be noted here that these lines of divergence run through

both monopoly and non-monopoly endogenous capital alike; although the fraction of the bourgeoisie interested in integration into the Common Market has certain specific features, it is not as if monopoly capital was exclusively tied to American capital, while non-monopoly capital was wholly oriented towards a European solution. In Greece and Spain, in particular, whole sections of monopoly capital have pursued a strategy of integration into the Common Market (the Union of Greek Industrialists, and Opus Dei in Spain).

Thus the principal effect that the contradictions between the United States and Europe had on these countries was that of producing an instability of hegemony for the power blocs, following from intensified struggle between fractions of their own bourgeoisies. The point is that the specific form of regime of these military dictatorships did not enable such contradictions to be regulated by the organic representation of these various fractions within the state apparatus; nor did it allow the establishment of a compromise equilibrium without serious upsets. But an equilibrium of this kind was still necessary for their political domination to function, in the context of intensified contradictions within these power blocs that were due, among other things, to the internationalization of capital and the contradictions between Europe and the United States as reflected within them. We can add here that the fall or decline of these regimes corresponded to a redistribution of the balance of forces within the power bloc in favour of the fraction of capital polarized towards the Common Market and at the expense of the fraction polarized towards the United States, whose interests these regimes preponderantly represented, though not exclusively. But this does not mean, at least as long as the situation of dependence is not radically eliminated (in which case the problem would not even arise), a clear and effective overthrow of the hegemony of a comprador capital tied to American capital (the military dictatorships) in favour of an endogenous capital tied to European capital (democratic regimes). Just as the contradiction between Europe and the United States is not explosive and antagonistic, neither is its reproduction within the power bloc translated into a contradiction of that kind. If I am anticipating somewhat here, this is simply to indicate already that it would be wrong to believe that the overthrow of the dictatorships in these countries signifies by itself a radical challenge to the role of American capital and the clear transition of the countries involved to some kind of European, 'third force' camp. These countries do not face a real choice between being 'American colonies' or being 'integrated into the Common Market'. The only solution for them is a process of independence and national liberation vis-à-vis imperialism as a whole.

2. Having said this, it would be wrong to discount, in the European attitude to the military dictatorships, the considerable role which the solidarity of the democratic and popular movements in the European countries, and public opinion there in general, has played, and continues to play, for the peoples of Portugal, Spain and Greece; this massive hostility towards the dictatorships bears no comparison with anything in the United States. It is this that is at the root of a certain reserve that the European governments have shown towards these regimes, and although this is not enough to explain the failure to integrate these countries into the Common Market, it has set a sort of preliminary condition to the commencement of such a process of integration, even though this process is itself still fraught with problems. While this enables the European governments to reap the full benefits of these countries' dependent situation without running the risks involved in complete integration, it does not mean that the sectors of the endogenous bourgeoisies interested in such an integration have not taken full account of a condition of this kind.

3. Finally, the contradictions between the United States and Europe are also reflected in the present differences on both diplomatic and military strategy, including those within NATO. One example of this is that of the differences between the United States and Europe over attitudes to the Israel-Arab conflict, and to some extent also attitudes towards the

oil-producing countries; a second involves differences on the problems of European defence and the Atlantic Alliance. I can not embark on an examination of these questions here, but it is evident that the contradictions between the United States and Europe are expressed today also in a partial challenge to the international strategy and diplomacy, and to the military defence policy, represented by the traditional concept and practice of the Atlantic Alliance, which were identified down to their smallest details with the strict political and economic interests of the United States.

On balance, however, taking the points so far made into consideration, it is clear that there is no question at the present time of Europe actually 'freeing' itself from an international strategy and a military alliance under the hegemony of the United States, particularly as there is not even a unified European position on these questions, but that what is involved is rather the acquisition of a certain margin of manoeuvre under this hegemony. The result of this is that Europe did not intervene actively for the overthrow of these military dictatorships allegedly 'exclusively tied' in this respect to the United States; the declarations of sympathy expressed by the French government after Greece left the NATO military organization (and in a manner that was more formal than anything else, at that) should not give rise to any illusions on this score. This is firstly because the present European governments, while systematically rejecting a policy of disarmament, are far from being able to effectively relieve American power in these countries. It is also because of the fear of the European bourgeoisies that an uncontrollable process might be set under way, leading to an eventual 'neutrality' of the countries affected, and thus considerably weakening NATO as a whole. Finally, and this particularly concerns the military regimes in these countries, if these regimes and their armies formed or still form major components of the American military deployment in Europe (Spain included), and are closely dependent on the United States, they were never mere pawns or stooges of American diplomatic and military strategy. A patent example of this is the overtly pro-Arab diplomacy of the Greek junta and the Franco regime, which bears on the specific interests of the bourgeoisies of these countries on the African continent. The contradictions between the United States and Europe in this field, and those within NATO in particular, did play a certain role in the overthrow or modification of these regimes, but this too is a role expressed in a particular fashion. These contradictions were reflected in the internal contradictions within the state apparatuses, and particularly within the army, which was always the principal apparatus for these regimes. This gave rise to internal divisions in the military apparatus between various groups and factions, certain of these upholding an indefatigable Atlanticism, others, on the other hand, standing for a diplomatic and military strategy more independent from the strict economic and political interests of the United States. These internal contradictions are manifest today in the armies of all European countries (we need only recall the debates on military strategy within the French army), and in the cases we are dealing with here they have had a considerable effect. Since the army functions as the bourgeoisie's *de facto* political party, in those countries where formalized political parties are banned by the military dictatorship, the contradictions within the bourgeoisie between capital with a European strategy and capital completely subordinated to the United States have been expressed in the army with particular intensity. The internal struggles of these fractions, especially those bearing on the role and function of NATO, have been particularly intense in the Greek, Portuguese and Spanish military apparatuses, and this contributed to the characteristic instability of the Greek and Portuguese regimes in their final phase.

After these remarks, which were intended both to demonstrate the primacy of 'internal factors' over 'external factors' and to demarcate the role of internal contradictions within the dictatorships' apparatuses as regards their overthrow or decay, we must now examine the specific strategy followed by the United States vis-à-vis these regimes.

Here, too, it is necessary to guard against simplistic

explanations. It is too clear to require any emphasis here that the United States has systematically and constantly supported these military regimes. In the Greek case, it even played a major role in its installation. But it would be equally false to draw the conclusion that the overthrow or decay of these regimes has proceeded despite or against the 'will' of the United States, as to believe the opposite conclusion that this has taken place at the United States' direct instigation. Because of the circumstances in which the change of regime took place, this second error has been particularly committed in the case of Greece. Several sectors of European public opinion saw Kissinger as sending Karamanlis back to Greece in order to democratize a regime that had become inconvenient, while the Communist Party of the Exterior and Andreas Papandreou also saw here at first the hand of the Americans, in their view however seeking to perpetuate 'monarcho-fascism' under a new facade.

Both these explanations neglect the specific weight of the internal factors, and in over-estimating the role of the United States, they also fail to recognize the specific orientation of American policy.

1. The United States certainly does have a global strategy in the present phase of imperialism, but it does not have just one single tactic; it rather has several tactics. The United States has a long experience in repressing the peoples of different countries, and in its role as gendarme of the Western bourgeoisies: it does not put all its eggs into one basket, and as far as strategy is concerned, does not stake everything on one single card.

The United States in fact always keeps several different cards in hand. Certainly, these cards are not all of equal value, and it prefers some of them to others; but it can often play different cards simultaneously. American strategy can therefore adapt itself to several possible solutions in the countries in its zone of dependence.

This is particularly clear in the scenario that took place in Greece, but it is equally so up to now in Portugal, or in the process now taking place in Spain. In Greece we have the following alternatives, in order of their preference by the United States:

(i) support almost to the end of the military dictatorship, though as this decayed it became less and less secure a war-horse in its specific form;
(ii) solution of an evolution of the dictatorship towards a 'legal' facade, which failed under Markezinis/Papadopoulos in 1973, but which could have been tried again;
(iii) solution of a more major political change, but one in which the military apparatus continued to maintain certain 'reserved domains';
(iv) Karamanlis solution;
(v) Kanellopoulos, a figure of the liberal right, far more open to the resistance organizations than Karamanlis;
(vi) solution of a transitional government under the aegis of the centre, with a vaguely right social-democratic character of the present German type; etc.

Analogous scenarios could be drawn up as far as Portugal is concerned, from support for the hard core of the dictatorship, through Caetano-ism with a liberal facade, through to and including a certain form of Spinola-ism or centrist govern-ment (viz. the ambiguity of American policy even after the fall of Spinola). In Spain, too, the different options could be listed.

It is true, certainly, that not all these solutions are supported by the United States with the same intensity, neither with the same constancy or by the same means; the United States attitude, confronted by a number of possible solutions that are 'acceptable', ranges from various degrees of support to the more or less passive acceptance of solutions that it con-siders the lesser evil – up to the point of a certain break. But this in itself shows how simplistic it is to view every change in the dependent countries that does not pass this breaking-point as due or at least corresponding to a conscious and unambiguous act of will on the part of the United States. To say that in Greece, for example, the Karamanlis solution corresponds to American 'intentions' is at the same time both true and false, in so far as this solution is for the United States simply one card among others, both ahead and behind certain others in its order of preference.

This polyvalent tactic of the United States is analogous to the similar tactic of the bourgeoisie in general as regards the forms of its political domination over the popular masses (the extreme case of a social-democratic government, for example, being pursued or at least tolerated by the bourgeoisies according to circumstances), and has both its advantages and its disadvantages. On the one hand, it enables the United States to perpetuate its domination under various forms that are adaptable to the concrete circumstances. On the other hand, forced as it is to multiply its tactics, and given the major weight of the internal factors in each country and above all that of the struggles of the popular masses, the risks of a skid, or total loss of control of a solution originally judged acceptable or even desirable, are many times greater. It frequently happens, then, in the present phase of a rise in popular struggles on a global scale, that the United States loses control of certain cards, to a lesser or greater extent. This is what particularly matters to us here, for the United States' loss of control is evident in the case of Portugal, and a certain skid has also taken place with Karamanlis over the Cyprus question.

A second element pertaining to the global strategy of the United States is also involved here. This concerns the extension of the spectrum of solutions judged acceptable or tolerable in this or that country, in a certain region of the world – particularly in Europe. As far as a particular country is concerned, this depends on the opportunities available to the United States for recapturing other countries in the same zone. This is particularly apparent in the case of Cyprus; after the failure of the Greek card (the colonels) to effect a partition of the island that would integrate it into NATO, the Americans played the Turkish card, successfully this time, in so far as the partition of the island, the chief goal sought, seems now to be a *fait accompli*. As far as the question of

NATO and American bases in the Mediterranean is concerned, the degree of escalation of United States policy against regimes liable to challenge its imperial prerogatives depends on the possibilities it has of shifting its bases to neighbouring countries. This explains, among other things, the fact that subsequent to the events in Portugal and Greece, and while those in Spain were still only predictable, the focus of American strategy in the Mediterranean shifted to Italy – not that this in any way means the United States has given up hope as far as Portugal and Greece are concerned.

2. This plurality of American tactics is not just the product of a conscious decision on their part; it is also related to the contradictions of American capital itself. Under-estimating the internal contradictions of the enemy, in fact, is just another way of over-estimating his strength. Internationalized American capital and the big American multinationals have major contradictions with those fractions of American capital whose base of accumulation and expansion is chiefly within the United States; there is thus a constant oscillation of American policy between an aggressive expansionism, which ultimately carries the day, and a permanent tendency towards a form of isolationism. There is also a further contradiction which does not completely coincide with the former, that between big monopoly capital and non-monopoly capital, which is still significant in the United States; this is expressed, among other things, in the particular way in which the American anti-trust laws operate, these having made difficulties only recently for multinational firms such as ITT and ATT, with a bad reputation. Given the specific form of the American political regime, these internal contradictions come to be translated into important contradictions within the state apparatuses. The peculiarity of the American state is that its 'external fascism', i.e. a foreign policy that generally does not hesitate to have recourse to the worst types of genocide, is embodied by institutions which, while far from representing an ideal case of bourgeois democracy (one need only recall the situation of social and national minorities in

the USA), still permit an organic representation of the various fractions of capital within the state apparatuses and the branches of the repressive apparatus. A regime of this kind, even though based on a real *union sacrée* of the great majority of the nation on major political objectives (and a lot could be said about this), is necessarily accompanied by constant and open contradictions within the state apparatuses.

These contradictions are precisely expressed in the divergent tactics simultaneously pursued by the different American state apparatuses involved in foreign policy. The CIA, the Pentagon and military apparatus, and the State Department often adopt different tactics, as do the Administration and executive branch as a whole as opposed to Congress; this is quite apparent in the cases of Greece, Portugal and Spain. What is more, these tactics are often pursued in parallel, giving rise to parallel networks that take no notice of each other and even combat one another. The case of the CIA and the Pentagon literally short-circuiting the State Department over the Cyprus question, or more recently in Portugal, provides a typical example of these practices. These contradictions also have their own specific effects, which accentuate the risk of skids; they are not just due to the deliberate multiplication of the tactics adopted in a particular case, but also to the parallel and divergent tactics resulting from the specific contradictions within the United States itself. Nothing would be more wrong, then, than to view the United States and its foreign policy as a monolithic bloc without its own internal fissures.

All these points finally lead to the same conclusions: not only do factors internal to the different countries in the United States' sphere of influence play the principal role in various conjunctures, but the very interventions of United States foreign policy leave these countries a certain margin of maneouvre, on account of the polyvalent tactics pursued and the contradictions crystallized in them, which relate in the last analysis to the internal contradictions of the enemy.

This margin of manoeuvre is extended today by the contradictory relations in Europe, and particularly in the

Mediterranean region, between East and West – the Soviet Union and the United States – which raises the subsidiary question of the role of the USSR in the changes of regime in the countries with which we are concerned.

In this case, too, we have to take account of a dual tendency.

In the first place, there is the understanding between the United States and the Soviet Union on maintaining the global balance of forces between them, as far as the spheres of influence of each of these two superpowers are concerned. Although this in no way means a status quo that is fixed in every detail as far as the internal situation in each country of the respective spheres of influence is concerned, it does mean that the two superpowers do everything in their power (which is far from being absolute) to prevent changes in one country from provoking a long-term upheaval in the balance of forces in the world, i.e. to prevent these changes from escaping the controlled readjustment of this balance.

As far as the attitude of the USSR and the Soviet-bloc countries towards the dictatorial regimes in Portugal, Spain and Greece is concerned, this has certainly been critical and negative, but this does not mean that the Soviet Union and its allies adopted, as states, a policy that effectively challenged these regimes. (This indeed is the least that one can say.) From Greece, where trade and diplomatic exchange with the Soviet bloc experienced a new upswing under the colonels' junta, through to Spain where a major development in economic relations is now under way, the score is clear enough.

All this, however, simply concerns the first aspect of the relations between the United States and the Soviet Union, and is sufficiently well-known not to need any emphasis here. The second aspect is far more important – this equilibrium in the balance of forces is a dynamic one, and highly unstable, as it in no way excludes considerable contradictions between the United States and the USSR. In point of fact, there is a permanent readjustment of this balance by way of the policy failures produced by these contradictions. The important factor in this respect is the direct presence of the USSR in the last few years, by way of the Israel-Arab conflict, as a power of the first order in a region that was previously a reserved domain of the United States. The Soviet presence in the Mediterranean is a constituent element of the new readjustment in the balance of forces, and it has major effects for the countries in this region. While provoking attempts by the United States to reinforce control of the NATO countries, it also makes massive and open American intervention in this region far more risky than this was previously, and this can undoubtedly have in Spain, as it already has had in Greece, highly positive effects on the circumstances in which the dictatorships are overthrown. We may say that the popular masses of these countries have been able to take advantage, or will be able to do so, of the contradictions between the United States and the Soviet Union, even though their path lies along a razor's edge, on account of the intensified efforts at control on the part of the United States. This situation could be seen at work in Greece in the Cyprus conflict, with the spectacular about-turns of the United States due among other things to the firm though cautious attitude of the Soviet Union, an attitude which made a massive American intervention in favour of the military junta altogether too risky.

III

The Dominant Classes

The fundamental question regarding the overthrow of the dictatorships in Portugal and Greece, and the changes impending in Spain, is the exact role played by the internal factors. More precisely, in what way have the so-called 'external' factors, the changes involved in the present phase of imperialism, been reproduced and internalized actually within the socio-economic and political structures of these countries?

The first point to consider here is that of the changes within the dominant classes of these countries. We must recall once again the points made as regards the new forms of dependence characterizing the relationships that certain dependent countries have with the imperialist centres: on the one hand, the rapid destruction of pre-capitalist modes and forms of production, on account of the forms assumed by the present imports of foreign capital in these countries; on the other hand, the process of dependent industrialization, due to the tendency of foreign capital to invest in the directly productive sectors of industrial capital, in the current context of internationalization of production and capital.

This permits the emergence or development of a new fraction of the bourgeoisie in these countries, which is very clear in the cases of Greece and Spain, and to a somewhat lesser extent also in Portugal: a fraction which I have referred to elsewhere as the domestic bourgeoisie. As this industrialization gets under way, there develop nuclei of an autochtonic bourgeoisie with a chiefly industrial character (directly productive capital), grafting itself onto this process in the domain of light industry in the consumer goods field, more occasionally in heavy industry (consumer durables, textiles, engineering, as well as steel and chemicals), and finally in the construction industries (cement, etc.). This is particularly the case, in Greece, with the domestic bourgeoisie organized in the Union of Greek Industrialists; in Portugal, with certain autochtonous capitals of the Lisbon/Setubal/Porto industrial belt, these capitals promoting the change in economic policy that was attempted, but failed, under Caetano, by R. Martins and his Fomento Industrial plan of 1972. In Spain, finally, the domestic bourgeoisie encompasses a large part of the autochtonic bourgeoisie, with the Catalan and Basque bourgeoisies in its lead, but also including a section of public capital under the control of the INI (National Industrialization Institute). These bourgeoisies are not simply confined to the industrial domain, but also extend to fields directly dependent on the industrialization process, such as transport, distribution (commercial capital), and even services of various kinds (particularly tourism). They are distinguished from earlier fractions of the bourgeoisie by the new complexity of their relationships with foreign capital.

Above all, they are distinguished from the comprador bourgeoisie, which is still very important in these countries. This comprador bourgeoisie (sometimes referred to as the 'oligarchy') can be defined as that fraction whose interests are entirely subordinated to those of foreign capital, and which functions as a kind of staging-post and direct intermediary for the implantation and reproduction of foreign capital in the countries concerned. The activity of this comprador bourgeoisie often assumes a speculative character, being concentrated in the financial, banking and commercial sectors, but it can also be found in the industrial sector, in those branches wholly dependent on and subordinated to foreign capital. In Greece, a typical case is that of shipping (Onassis, Niarchos, etc.), and capital invested in marine construction, petrol refineries, etc. In Portugal, the small number of big comprador groups (CUF, Espirito Santo, Borges e Irmao, Portugues do Atlantico, etc.) centre around banking, and while controlling a large part of autochtonic production, they are at the same time oriented to the exploitation of the African colonies – being closely tied to foreign capital both in Portugal and in its colonies. In Spain, finally, there is the characteristic case of a very substantial banking and financial comprador sector (industrial banks in particular), and industries that directly depend on it. From the political point of view, this bourgeoisie is the true support and agent of foreign imperialist capital.

The domestic bourgeoisie on the other hand, although dependent on foreign capital, also has significant contradictions with it. This is principally because it is cheated in its share of the cake, as far as the exploitation of the masses is concerned; the lion's share of the surplus-value goes to foreign capital and its agents the comprador bourgeoisie, at the domestic bourgeoisie's expense. There is also the fact that since the domestic bourgeoisie is concentrated chiefly in the industrial sector, it is interested in an industrial development less polarized towards the exploitation of the country by foreign capital, and in a state intervention which would guarantee it its protected markets at home, while also making it more competitive vis-à-vis foreign capital. It seeks an extension and development of the home market by a certain increase in the purchasing power and consumption of the masses, which would supply it with a greater market outlet, and also seeks state aid to help it develop its exports.

It must still be made clear – and this is very important as far as this domestic bourgeoisie's policy towards the dictatorships is concerned – that it is not a genuine national bourgeoisie, i.e. a bourgeoisie that is really independent of foreign capital and which could take part in an anti-imperialist struggle for effective national independence, such as sometimes did exist in these countries in the past (in Spain above all), during the earlier phases of imperialism. The development of this domestic bourgeoisie coincides with the internationalization of labour processes and production, and with the internationalization of capital, in other words with the induced reproduction of the dominant relations of production actually within these various social formations. By this fact alone, while its existence involves certain contradictions with foreign capital, this domestic bourgeoisie is to a certain extent itself dependent on the processes of internationalization under the aegis of foreign capital: dependent on technological processes and labour productivity, on a complex network of sub-contraction for foreign capital, on the sector of light industry and consumer goods in which it is frequently confined in this sector's relationships with heavy industry (the privileged sector for foreign multinational corporations), as well as on commercial outlets. This explains, among other things, the political weakness of this domestic bourgeoisie, which, although it tries to translate into political action its contradictions with foreign capital and the big comprador bourgeoisie, is unable, for the most part, to wield long-term political hegemony over the other fractions of the bourgeoisie and the dominant classes, i.e. over the power bloc.

Two other important characteristics should be added to this.

a) The domestic bourgeoisie does not fall entirely on one side of the divide between monopoly and non-monopoly capital. While the domestic bourgeoisie does include a section of non-monopoly capital in the countries with which we are concerned (the 'small and medium-size firms'), it also includes entire segments of monopoly capital; and conversely, there are also segments of non-monopoly capital entirely subordinated to foreign capital by way of sub-contracting agreements and commercial channels. Thus although the domestic bourgeoisie exhibits a certain political unity in its contradictions with foreign capital, it is itself deeply divided, particularly in so far as it is cleft by the contradiction between monopoly and non-monopoly capital, and this fact is not without effect on its political weakness.

b) Since the domestic bourgeoisie is itself still relatively dependent on foreign capital, the contradictions between the various foreign capitals in these countries, particularly those between United States capital and capital from the

Common Market, and between capitals from different fractions of internationalized capital (industrial, banking, commercial), are all reflected and reproduced actually within the domestic bourgeoisie itself, according to the divergent lines of dependence that cut across it. The domestic bourgeoisie is marked by the same 'externally centred' character as the entire economy of these countries, which is polarized towards a process of internationalization under the aegis of capital from the dominant countries. And this is always a factor in the political weakness of this bourgeoisie.

It should now be clear that the distinction between domestic bourgeoisie and comprador bourgeoisie is not based on a simplistic distinction between a bourgeoisie 'isolated' and 'enclosed' in its own national space and an internationalized bourgeoisie, i.e. on a spatial distinction, but rather on the process of internationalization of capital, its various moments, phases and turns as they are expressed in each social formation. The distinction between comprador and domestic bourgeoisie, while being based on the new structure of dependence, is not a statistical and empirical distinction, fixed rigidly once and for all. It is rather a tendential differentiation, the concrete configuration it takes depending to a certain extent on the conjuncture. This capital or that, this or that fraction of capital, industrial branch or enterprise, originally tied to foreign capital, may in this process acquire a relative autonomy and gradually come to take its place in the ranks of the domestic bourgeoisie, just as, in the opposite direction, capitals that were originally autochtonic may gradually fall under the thumb of foreign capital – a process of constant reclassification which must always be taken into account.

This phenomenon of the domestic bourgeoisie does not just affect Spain, Greece and, to a somewhat lesser extent, Portugal. It can be found in the majority of European countries, on account of the peculiar and complex dependence of Europe vis-à-vis the United States. But there are significant differences between the domestic bourgeoisies of the European imperialist countries and those of the countries that the main dividing line of the imperialist chain locates on the side of the dominated. These bourgeoisies not only have a far weaker economic base than do the domestic bourgeoisies of the other European countries; they are also marked by an ideological and political weakness, in countries where the introduction and development of capitalism took place on the basis of a very slender endogenous base of primitive accumulation (Portugal, Spain), or even entirely under the aegis of foreign capital (Greece). A notable fact in this regard was the inability of the Portuguese, Spanish and Greek bourgeoisies to carry through their own bourgeois-democratic revolutions. One must of course reject the ideal-type model of bourgeois-democratic revolution against which these 'failures' are measured – a model whose political imagery somehow blends together the French Revolution with the results of the English Revolution: a French Revolution without its various Bonapartes, as it were. It is hardly necessary to recall that such a model has never existed, and measured against it, all the bourgeois-democratic revolutions have to a certain extent 'failed' or been wanting. In the final analysis, they never existed at all. But it is none the less true that, if we examine what has happened in these countries in relation to the other European countries (including Germany), the differences are clear: they are expressed in particular in the characteristic inability of the Portuguese and Spanish bourgeoisies, and to a somewhat lesser extent also the Greek, to establish a bourgeois-ideological discourse with a hegemonic character in their social formations, and in their difficulties of political organization which are equally specific to these countries. These characteristics still weigh very heavily on the domestic bourgeoisies.

Nevertheless, this domestic bourgeoisie still played an important part in the change of regime in Greece and in Portugal; it will be equally important in the process that we can foresee in Spain. What is beyond doubt in all three cases is that gradually, if in different degrees, broad sectors of the domestic bourgeoisie distanced themselves from the military dictatorship (or are doing so now in the Spanish case), and withdrew their support from it. Broad sectors of the comprador bourgeoisies, on the other hand, supported these regimes till the end, if to a varying extent and by complex tactics. We must now study this aspect of the problem, taking into account the specific characteristics of the domestic bourgeoisies.

1. In the first place, these regimes overwhelmingly promoted the interests of the comprador bourgeoisie, in the long run, leading to a clearly visible subordination to foreign capital, American in particular, until this ultimately finished by seriously inconveniencing the domestic bourgeoisies.

It would be wrong to see these bourgeoisies as constantly and systematically bullied by the military regimes, themselves mere 'pawns' of foreign capital, so that their attitude was always one of constant, open and unambiguous opposition to the regime in question. Besides the advantages that these bourgeoisies themselves drew from the 'domestic peace', the Greek and Spanish regimes often promoted and sometimes even sought their development. The domestic bourgeoisie thus formed part of the power bloc corresponding to the dictatorships, and on top of this, in the Greek case, this bourgeoisie had itself clearly supported the actual establishment of the military dictatorship in 1967, tailing behind the comprador bourgeoisie, in the face of the rise of popular struggles and a break in the representational tie with its political representatives. But the development of the domestic bourgeoisies under these regimes, essentially due to the internationalization of capital, revived their contradictions with the comprador bourgeoisie, and was the source of their growing reserve towards the dictatorships, whose organic relationship to the comprador bourgeoisie and to foreign capital had become in the meantime too narrow a yoke.

The domestic bourgeoisie thus demanded a growing share of state support, i.e. that the state should take more account of its own particular interests. It sought to readjust the compromise with the big comprador bourgeoisie within the power bloc, and in this way to acquire a political weight appropriate to its place in society. Moreover, in the case of Spain, and particularly that of Portugal, it sought to break the very configuration of this power bloc, characterized by a close alliance between the comprador bourgeoisie and the large landowners, by challenging the weight of the agrarian interest, which had become disproportionate. In Spain, the stabilization plan of 1959 had to a certain extent already reduced the political weight of the landlords to the benefit of the comprador bourgeoisie, and the same thing had happened to a much smaller extent in Portugal between 1950 and 1960. The weight of the landlords, which was related to the very origin of the Spanish and Portuguese regimes, not only no longer corresponded to their economic position, already on the wane, but was ever more of a brake on the process of industrialization. Because of the accentuated contradictions between agriculture and industry in the development of this dependent capitalism, industrialization could only proceed to the massive detriment of the countryside. All these factors made the contradiction between industrial capital (the domestic bourgeoisie) and the landlords far more severe than that between the landlords and banking capital, the sector in which the comprador bourgeoisie has generally been concentrated in Portugal, and even more so in Spain. (Things were different in Greece, on account of the much earlier liquidation of large landed property.)

This situation as a whole, therefore, also led to a deepening of the contradictions within the power bloc itself, and hence to the need for a form of state which would permit their negotiated and on-going resolution by way of an organic representation of the various classes and class fractions of the power bloc, i.e. through their own political organizations.

The domestic bourgeoisie long held out the hope that a process of this kind would be set under way by the dictatorships themselves, by way of a few minor adjustments in the direction of 'normalization' or 'liberalization' of the type followed by Papadopoulos/Markezinis, Caetano, Opus Dei or, more recently, Arias Navarro – an internal evolution of these regimes which however proved impossible. To understand its attitude towards the dictatorships, we must pay attention to the real policy of the domestic bourgeoisie, and not confine ourselves to the attitude of its traditional political representatives. Certain of these, in fact, in Spain and particularly in Greece, have long since been far more far-sighted, some of them having long ago taken up a position of opposition (the case of Carlism in Spain for the Basque bourgeoisie), others remaining in opposition from the start of the dictatorship (the Centre Union party in Greece, and even certain prominent individuals in Karamanlis's old party, the National Radical Union). But the crisis of representation between the domestic bourgeoisie and its traditional representatives, which was part of the original basis for these dictatorships, left the domestic bourgeoisie lagging behind its representatives, right up to the moment when experience proved the impossibility of an internal evolution by the regime – the moment when the tie of representation began to be established 'against' these regimes.

The most important thing here is to note briefly, already at this point, why these regimes were unable to permit the solutions desired by the domestic bourgeoisie. It is true that military dictatorships are not monolithic blocs: the various apparatuses and branches of these regimes certainly allow the different components of the power bloc to be present within the state, reflecting the contradictions between them as internal contradictions of the regime, and particularly of its dominant apparatus, the armed forces. But the specific structure of these regimes and their apparatuses did not in this conjuncture allow the regulated and orderly functioning of class representation. The elimination of the various political organizations of the power bloc itself (the political parties), the rigidity of the apparatuses and the parallelism between their branches, the spasmodic shifts in the sites of real power, the suppression of civil liberties, and the shift in the role of organic representatives of the bourgeoisie in favour of 'camarillas' and 'clans' whose members were often of peasant or petty-bourgeois origin (army and state administration) – all this led more and more to conflicts within the power bloc

being settled by sudden blows, jerkily, and behind the scenes.
There was a prodigious lack of coherence (viz. the complaint
of 'incompetence' that the bourgeoisie levels at these regimes)
which not only precluded contradictions from being settled
politically, but eventually even threatened the organized
hegemony of the bourgeoisie as such.

The comprador bourgeoisie and the big landowners,
furthermore, were ensconced in impregnable fiefs. In the
Greek case, in particular, this situation perpetuated that
already existing before the dictatorship, when the comprador
bourgeoisie already had at its disposal a 'para-state' apparatus
in the form of the palace and army, which functioned as an
effective dual power parallel with the legal government. If the
dictatorships originally managed, and even for quite some
time, to appease the crisis of representation that affected
relationships between the various fractions of the power bloc
and their specific political representatives, and to set themselves up as the restorers of hegemony, they could not in the
long run play this role with respect to the domestic bourgeoisie.
This fraction, both because of its conflict with the comprador
bourgeoisie and its efforts to readjust the balance of forces to
its own advantage, and also because of its particular relationship with the popular masses, realized that it needed an
independent representation and an autonomous political
organization; it attempted to achieve this within these
regimes by way of the press and publishing (hence a relative
'liberalization'), but this came to a dead end. What happened
was that any attempt at such a liberalization was immediately
transformed into a open breach for the popular masses and
their organizations. Experience proved that, on account of the
specific organizational structure of these regimes and their
organic relationship with the big comprador bourgeoisie, the
domestic bourgeoisie could only organize itself through an
apparatus that was marginal to the regime's own structures,
and this the regime would not tolerate. Any marginal apparatus of this kind was rapidly transformed into a bastion against
it.

Certain characteristics of this process need to be indicated in more detail. It cannot be seen as a struggle by the domestic bourgeoisie to conquer effective hegemony within the power bloc, in other words as a long-term shift in hegemony away from the big comprador bourgeoisie. This domestic bourgeoisie is not a genuine national bourgeoisie; it remains economically weak, divided by internal contradictions and dependent on foreign capital, and this is why it also exhibits very clear limitations on the political and ideological levels. Its opposition to the dictatorships was always hesitant and vacillating, and if it should ultimately prove able to recapture the leadership of the democratization process, this would in no way mean that a genuine process of national independence had been set under way; all that this involved would be a rearrangement of the relationship between the domestic bourgeoisie, foreign capital and the comprador bourgeoisie, in favour of the domestic bourgeoisie, but still in the longer term under the renegotiated hegemony of the comprador bourgeoisie. This is precisely what is now happening in Greece. The Karamanlis government has set itself up as the political broker of the entire Greek bourgeoisie, on the basis of a new compromise between the domestic and comprador fractions, a compromise in which the political programme of the principal bourgeois opposition party, the Centre Union – traditional representative of the domestic bourgeoisie – is simply one possible variant. In Spain, the same readjustment, which was attempted within the regime itself by the Opus Dei episode, but miscarried, is already present in outline in the opposition to the dictatorship.

Certain sectors of the big comprador bourgeoisie, aware of the risk that the dictatorships represent to the exercise of their hegemony within the power bloc, themselves began to play the card of a certain 'de-fascisization', at a certain stage, while still continuing to support these regimes, and this enabled them to keep the terrain of compromise with the domestic bourgeoisie permanently open. But there is here a clear distinction from the situation of the domestic bourgeoisie; in the latter case, there was a long-run and strategic opposition to the regime related to genuine structural reasons, while for the comprador bourgeoisie this is simply a reserve tactic, parallel to its main policy of support for these regimes right to the bitter end. Only in Portugal, with the failure of the colonial war and its sequels, did certain sectors of the big comprador bourgeoisie start to seek an escape route from the existing regime (Spinola). But here too, the contradictions between these sectors and the domestic bourgeoisie soon burst into the open.

These are precisely the elements within the power bloc in the dictatorships to which the contradictions between American and European capital discussed in the previous chapter were articulated. It is now possible to examine the induced reproduction of these contradictions and their particular articulation to the social forces within the countries involved. At the risk of a certain schematism, we can say that it is particularly certain important sectors of the domestic bourgeoisie that have turned towards a policy of integration into the Common Market. It would be wrong for all that to see this attitude on the part of the domestic bourgeoisie as corresponding to a policy of genuine national independence, guaranteed by the structures of the Common Market to its member countries. This is essentially due to the fact that the big comprador bourgeoisies, in Spain and Greece above all, are organically tied to American capital, and by ties far closer than those affecting the domestic bourgeoisies. But as the latter are incapable of leading a process of national independence, they have seen in the Common Market the possibility of countering the big comprador bourgeoisie, and of shifting the weight of dependence, as it were, towards another party that would be more favourable to their interest and enable them to readjust the balance of forces to their advantage. Taking into account what we have already said about the United States/Common Market relationship, this would signify no more than the replacement of the direct hegemony of the United States in these countries by its indirect hegemony – mediated, as it were, by the contradictions between the United States and the Common Market. This would be a readjustment of relations between American capital and this domestic bourgeoisie – a fraction moreover, which, in its own national context, inclines towards the democratization of the regime as its preferred solution.

The conjunction of these two factors is the context in which we have to situate the relationship between the democratization of the dictatorships and the integration of these countries into the Common Market, both as regards the policy of these bourgeoisies towards the Common Market, and the EEC policy towards their regimes. The dictatorships had long represented above all else the interests of the big comprador bourgeoisie, and were thus 'too subordinate' to American strategy. However we should remember that it is wrong either to see the simple fact of this subordination as itself the cause of a certain reticence towards them on the part of the European governments (we need only think of Britain or West Germany), or to see these regimes as simple 'pawns' of their comprador bourgeoisies, and thereby of American imperialism. The dictatorships themselves sought, on occasion, integration into the Common Market, by way of their relationships to their domestic bourgeoisies. But apart from what has already been said on the reticence of the European bourgeoisies to grant these countries full EEC membership (the Common Agricultural Policy), these efforts were made at a time when the nature of the dictatorships blocked the development of the domestic bourgeoisie itself, the Common Market's war-horse in these countries by virtue of the European bourgeoisies' contradictions with American capital. This explains among other things the contradictory attitudes of these domestic bourgeoisies. While pressing for integration into the Common Market, they requested the European bourgeoisies not to allow such an integration without changes in the nature of the regimes.

The contradictions between the big comprador bourgeoisie and the domestic bourgeoisie, and the induced reproduction of the contradictions between the United States and Common Market, are thus articulated to and focussed in the privileged centre of the national state, and therefore the form of its regime. If this is to be understood, we must not lose sight of the fact that the present phase of imperialism, and the increased internationalization of capital and production, in no way detract from the role of the national state in the accumulation of capital – contrary to what has often been said. The process of internationalization is certainly not a process taking place 'over the heads' of these states, so that the role of the national states would either be replaced by that of 'economic powers', or else imply the birth of an effective supranational state (United Europe or the American superstate). If this were the case, it would be impossible to understand how and why this internationalization, and the internal contradictions it has produced within the power blocs of the countries with which we are concerned, are focussed on the question of the national state and its form of regime. National states are still the nodal points of the internationalization process, which actually increases their decisive role in the accumulation of capital (particularly by way of their economic functions), and this explains why they are still more than ever the privileged object of struggle in the conflicts between the various fractions of the bourgeoisie itself. If this were not the case, then the form of regime in these national states would be a matter of complete indifference for these bourgeoises and their component fractions. It is necessary to draw attention here to the particularly important economic role of the state in Portugal, Spain (the INI) and Greece, as a specific characteristic of dependent industrialization on a weak basis of endogenous primitive accumulation. In cases of this kind, because of the economic weakness of the domestic bourgeoisie, the question of the distribution of state subsidies becomes a major issue in its contradictions with the comprador bourgeoisie. (In Portugal, some 50 per cent of the state budget was devoted to the colonial wars, in the interest of the comprador bourgeoisie.)

Nevertheless, these national states must undergo considerable changes if they are to take charge of the internationalization of capital that is actually being reproduced within their own social formations. And this is why the contradictions of this internationalization process, as they are expressed – as always – within their own power blocs, cut right through the states in question, and form an important element in changes in the form of regime.

2. This directly leads on to the second reason for the progressive disaffection of the domestic bourgeoisies of these countries with their dictatorships, which bears on the relationships between these bourgeoisies – and the regimes themselves – and the popular masses.

The first thing to note here is that the same reasons that gave rise to the genesis and development of the domestic bourgeoisie (dependent industrialization), also produced far-reaching upheavals in the socio-economic structures of these countries. Given the particular form of regime, this process was accompanied by a very definite development of mass struggles.

Now the policy of the domestic bourgeoisie towards the popular masses, and towards the working class in particular, gradually came to differentiate itself from that of the comprador bourgeoisie which the regimes in question primarily expressed; it has evolved towards more open and conciliatory positions with regard to their demands. This policy is also different from the policy of the multinational corporations in this respect, which in certain 'industrialized' countries can often afford to be conciliatory as far as wage rises are concerned. Located as they are in leading sectors, the multinationals can more easily make up for their losses by an increased productivity of labour, though in the countries we are concerned with here they too followed a characteristic low-wage policy.

This difference in the policy of the domestic bourgeoisie is due above all to the fact that, concentrated as it is in the industrial sector, while not having as the multinationals do the possibility of rapidly shifting production from one country to another, it is in the direct line of fire of the violent agitation endemic to this sector. Given the inability of the dictatorships to contain this agitation by mere repression, the domestic bourgeoisie is ever more inclined to accept trade-unionism as a fact of life, for the sake of acquiring genuinely representative spokesmen to negotiate with, and thereby embarking on a process of resolving its conflicts with the working class. One manifest demonstration of this has been the attitude of a section of the Spanish employers to the workers' commissions in Spain, while the Union of Greek Industrialists also supported plans to 'democratize' the regime's official unions, and a wing of the Portuguese bosses, too, accepted the direct election of delegates by the base, within the corporatist unions of the Estado Novo. The domestic bourgeoisie is also interested in an endogenous industrialization, and because of the structural difficulties that this presents, it implies an effective ideological and political mobilization of the working class and the popular masses, which these regimes are incapable of carrying through. They are in fact distinguished from the classical fascist regimes (of the German or Italian type) by their inability to develop genuine mass movements. They remained isolated from the popular masses, and above all from the working class, never managing to implant themselves in it at all seriously. In such a context, the policy of concessions to the working class makes up for this deficiency of the dictatorships, as far as the domestic bourgeoisie is concerned.

On top of this, the domestic bourgeoisies sought to win the support of the popular masses and the working class in their own struggle against either a comprador-agrarian bloc (Portugal and Spain) or simply against the comprador bourgeoisie (Greece). For the sake of this, they were ready to pay the price of democratization, particularly as this democratization also met their own aspirations, as the only way to readjust the balance of forces within the power bloc to their relative advantage.

It is true that the domestic bourgeoisie only gradually came round to these positions, following the successive defeats of various attempts at normalization that would have permitted it to have the advantages of ending the dictatorship without the associated risks: the increased possibilities for popular struggle in the democratic regimes. In point of fact, however, these regimes were doubly inconvenient for the domestic bourgeoisie. On the one hand, it was often forced, given its own isolation in the face of working-class struggle, to give in to economic demands; the increased exploitation of the working class was chiefly a relative increase, compared with the stupendous rise in profits, rather than an absolute one, and working-class wages often advanced significantly in terms of real purchasing power. On the other hand, the domestic bourgeoisie never drew any long-term political advantage from the concessions it made to the working class; the political rigidity towards the popular masses that was an organic feature of these regimes meant that working-class opposition to them remained unassuaged.

It should be added here, for all that, that both in its struggles against the big comprador bourgeoisie and in its particular relationship to the popular masses, it was the monopoly sectors of the domestic bourgeoisie that took the lead, towing the non-monopoly sectors in their wake. This was clearest of all at the beginning of the Portuguese events (Spinola), but also in Greece (the policy of the Union of Greek Industrialists), and in the process now under way in Spain, where it is these monopoly sectors in particular who are keenest on an alliance with the Communist Party (viz. the *Junta Démocratica*), rather than the non-monopoly sectors. What is true for integration into the Common Market (which suits the monopoly sectors of the domestic bourgeoisie far more than its non-monopoly sectors), also applies to the search for a policy of negotiation with the working class; it is easier for the monopoly sectors of the domestic bourgeoisie to pay the price for the support of the popular masses in their opposition to the comprador bourgeoisie, than for the non-monopoly sectors to do so. The domestic bourgeoisie's opposition to the dictatorships has so far been led by its monopoly sectors, and guided by their political perspectives, these sectors being modestly known as the 'enlightened' or 'neo-capitalist' bourgeoisie.

A situation fraught with implications, and an explosive situation at that.

The arguments advanced above at least explain one
dominant fact: the dictatorships have gradually seen a
conjunctural and tactical convergence of interests between
the domestic bourgeoisie on the one hand, and the working
class and popular masses on the other, its objective being the
replacement of these regimes by 'democratic' ones. This was
the fundamental locus of convergence, even if it also implies,
as the basis of the compromise involved, a certain limitation
of the prerogatives exercized up to now by foreign capital
and the comprador bourgeoisie, a certain move away from
a foreign policy too subordinate to American imperialist
strategy, and an improvement in the material conditions of the
popular masses. All these elements can be seen at work in the
present policy of the Karamanlis government in Greece. This
is certainly a real development, but it has not gone any further
than that. In no sense and at no point has there been any
convergence or agreement that would signify, on the part of
the domestic bourgeoisie, the beginnings of a real struggle
for national independence; there have not even been, up to
now, any far-reaching democratic and social reforms, even of
a simple anti-monopoly type. The proof of this, again, is the
process followed up to now in Greece, the programme of the
Democratic Junta in Spain, and *negatively*, the frictions and
contradictions on this score that have arisen in Portugal,
and which are still far from being settled. All these factors can
only be understood if account is taken of the characteristics
that prevent this domestic bourgeoisie from becoming an
effective national bourgeoisie, in particular its heterogeneity,
its division due to the contradictions that run through it, and
its political and ideological weakness and ambiguity.

Events in Greece and Portugal, therefore, as we shall
examine in more detail below, are far from proving the
possibilities often ascribed to them of a strategic alliance
between the popular masses and fractions of the bourgeoisie
on the basis of a process of national liberation and transition
to socialism – as if these were genuine national bourgeoisies.
They prove exactly the opposite, and the same is true of the
process now unfolding in Spain. And if it could already be

predicted in advance that no fractions of the bourgeoisie would be found ready to support a process of transition to socialism, there has not even been any sign up to now of any fractions ready to support even limited anti-monopoly objectives such as are contained in the 'Common Programme' of the French Communist and Socialist Parties. (In Greece, the Karamanlis government certainly does not support these, but neither does the Centre Union.)

Without being negligible, these objectives still do not add up to a real process of national liberation and transition to socialism, so that in certain circumstances they might possibly be accepted by fractions of the bourgeoisie. What we do have in the countries under consideration here, though, is a highly significant phenomenon that bears precisely on these countries' peculiarities, and basically therefore on the dictatorial form of regime which they have experienced: a genuine tactical alliance between broad sectors of the domestic bourgeoisie and the popular forces on a precise and limited objective, i.e. the overthrow of the military dictatorships and their replacement by 'democratic' regimes. We should also remember the other element peculiar to these countries, that it is precisely the monopoly sectors of the domestic bourgeoisie that have been the spearhead of its progressive opposition to these regimes, only drawing after them the non-monopoly sectors.

Two problems can be dealt with here. The less important of the two is whether the main resistance organizations of the popular masses, and the Communist Parties in particular, were correct to accept, as they all did do, an alliance with the domestic bourgeoisies, either explicitly formulated or at least *de facto*, with the precise and limited objective of over-throwing the dictatorships? The answer to this is an incontest-able 'yes'. To defeat fascism, as Trotsky well said, one must make alliance with the devil himself. In point of fact, however, the divergences that arose within the major wing of the resist-ance came increasingly to bear, not on whether a tactical alliance of this kind *should* be made, but rather on whether it *could* be, in other words if this was not just chasing after phantoms. Could the domestic bourgeoisie be an ally, even on this precise and limited objective? Did its interests really lead it to support the overthrow of the regime? The answer to this was very far from clear to everyone involved, but the facts have shown that, in the particular conjuncture in these countries, this was in fact the case.

The second point is far more important: under whose hegemony is this alliance to be made? For there is no point in denying that, in the conjuncture of the overthrow of the dictatorships, it has been made under the hegemony of the domestic bourgeoisie, whether directly and clearly, as in Greece and Spain, or as yet more hesitantly and more contested, as in Portugal. This clearly means that, even if this bourgeoisie does not have effective leadership of the struggles in progress, and even if the overthrow of the dictatorships significantly aids the present and future struggles of the popular masses, the process has so far developed to a large extent, if not completely, to the benefit of the bourgeoisie's political interests. The inevitable corollary of this is that the process of democratization has not been telescoped together with a process of transition to socialism and national liberation. This in turn raises a further question: was such a telescoping at all possible, in the world conjuncture and given the objective conditions in these countries, or worse still, did the process of democratization only become possible in so far as a telescoping of this kind was excluded. (The precise meaning of this 'telescoping' process is that a specific stage of democratization is dispensed with.) To put this another way, in political terms: given the articulation within these countries of the contradictions imperialist dependence/national liberation, capitalism/socialism, and dictatorship/democracy, was it not really this last contradiction that gradually became the principal contradiction governing the beginnings of the democratization process, partly because of the new class realities that it concealed, and partly because of the relative defeat of the working class and its organizations in their bid to play a hegemonic role in this conjuncture?

In answering these questions I shall stick to the example of

Portugal, which might seem to offer the biggest problem for the argument I have suggested.

We should note first of all that, even during the period that has followed the eviction of Spinola, the anti-monopoly declarations of the Armed Forces Movement have not been accompanied by the slightest attempt at their realization; the arrest or dismissal of a few figures responsible for economic sabotage in no way amounts to an effective implementation of anti-monopoly measures. The anti-monopoly declarations of the first Armed Forces Movement programme were in any case extremely vague, as the product of a compromise within the AFM itself, which was deeply divided on this question. At all events, during the overthrow of the regime and the period that followed, no popular alliance was concluded even on an anti-monopoly programme roughly comparable with the Common Programme of the French left, let alone one of a transition to socialism.

What is the significance in this context of the crisis of July 1974 (dismissal of the then prime minister Palma Carlos and his replacement by Colonel Gonçalves), and the subsequent removal from power of General Spinola? It must be stressed here that during the first phase of the old regime's overthrow (the April revolution), even sectors of the big comprador bourgeoisie (the Champalimaud group for example), including certain big international firms, supported Spinola. The failure of the colonial war had converted them to his neo-colonial plan as presented in *Portugal and its Future*, and convinced them that this was the only way to perpetuate the exploitation of the colonies. Other sectors, however, such as the Espirito Santo group, strongly rooted in Angola, maintained their policy of support for the colonial war. This is the basis on which the compromise of this first phase was reached, between the domestic bourgeoisie and the neo-colonialist sectors of the comprador bourgeoisie, the latter being strongly represented in Spinola's first government and the organs of power that existed at that time, including the Junta of National Salvation.

The contradictions between the comprador bourgeoisie on

the one hand, the domestic bourgeoisie and popular forces on the other, came to a head over the colonial question above all, but also over the issue of civil and political liberty. At its first stage, this crisis led to the dismissal of Palma Carlos in July 1974, and his replacement by Colonel Gonçalves, already marking a turn in the reorganization of the balance of forces in the power bloc to the detriment of the big comprador bourgeoisie. However the game of compromise between the domestic and comprador bourgeoisie continued during the period of the Second Provisional Government; measures favouring the popular masses were certainly taken (increase in the minimum wage to 3,300 escudos, still well below the 6,000 escudos demanded by the opposition under the Caetano regime), but the government's economic programme published on 18th August was nothing more on the whole than a classical programme of austerity, and was far from envisaging any anti-monopoly measures – to say nothing here of the almost total absence of agrarian reform. On 22nd August, moreover, the representatives of the big comprador bourgeoisie, including Jose Manuel de Melo, the major shareholder in the CUF, Manuel Ricardo Espirito Santo and Antonio Champalimaud paid a visit to Gonçalves and presented him with their five-year plan for a 'modern, developed and progressive capitalism', envisaging the creation of 100,000 new jobs and investment of the order of 120 million escudos.

It was in September, however, after the eviction of Spinola, that the domestic bourgeoisie began to strengthen its relative position within the power bloc, in parallel with a consolidation of the popular movement. This was undoubtedly a highly unstable situation. The domestic bourgeoisie continued to support the 'Portuguese experiment', even after the departure of Spinola, but was far from having been won over to anti-monopoly measures. I need only give the example of the *Le Monde* interview with Dr Cabral, from the executive commission of the CIP (Confederation of Portuguese Industrialists), which includes some 40,000 Portuguese firms among its members. (This was on 17th December 1974, i.e.

well after the fall of Spinola.) Dr Cabral, while he proclaimed himself a convinced supporter of the democratization process (the interview's title is 'We Will Not Be the Pinochets of the Portuguese Economy') and the relative 'amelioration' of working-class conditions, also attacking certain foreign firms (ITT, Sogantal, etc.), declared: 'Added to this there is also the problem of the necessary reconversion of a large number of small and medium-sized firms. This is a banner that the left-wing parties have seized upon, in a demagogic way. As we see it, it would run contrary to the spirit of the April 25th revolution to promote the artificial survival of firms inherited from the old regime, with its protectionist policies, if they are not economically viable.'

The emergency economic programme of February 1975, drawn up under the guidance of Melo Antunes, a leading member of the AFM, was the fruit of a difficult compromise, but follows in the same path as that of the previous August. It is in all essentials a programme of austerity, even though it does envisage the possibility of certain very limited national-izations. (Even supposing that these were actually carried out, they would still leave Portugal well behind France, Italy, Britain or West Germany in this respect, given the almost total absence, up till now, of a public sector.) What is more, room has been left for compromise with certain sectors of the comprador bourgeoisie. This appears in the repeated state-ments by political leaders of the AFM itself (Carvalho, Gonçalves, Costa Gomes) in favour of foreign investment in Portugal and guaranteeing its protection on behalf of the new regime, which has formally ruled out the possibility of nationalizing such investment, even though its economic programme certainly restricts somewhat the exorbitant privileges enjoyed up till now by foreign capital, by establish-ing 'control' mechanisms similar to those existing in other European countries. Given the characteristic dependence of Portugal on foreign capital, it is clear that not just a process of transition to socialism, but even an effective 'anti-monopoly' policy, could not be carried through without radical anti-imperialist measures.

The specific characteristics of the Portuguese case, however, also involve the power of the popular movement and the weakness of the domestic bourgeoisie, compared with the situation in Greece and Spain; this is why its hegemony has been less clear-cut and highly contested, in a permanent imbalance of forces, even during the realization of what still certainly remains a 'democratic stage'. We should not dwell simply on the spectacular role of the Portuguese Communist Party and the most radical fraction of the AFM. For the domestic bourgeoisie (and even, to a lesser extent, certain sections of the comprador bourgeoisie) is very well represented at the present time within the 'progressive' forces in Portugal.

This is the case above all in the armed forces. The AFM only embraces some 400 officers (the delegates and the 'historic nucleus'), out of the 4000 that the three services have altogether. A large number of these (the 'professionalist' tendency, several officers close to the Socialist Party) follow the representative of the traditional hierarchy, the 'moderate' President Costa Gomes, former defence under-secretary and commander-in-chief of the Portuguese army under the Estado Novo in its Caetano period. Not only does Costa Gomes act as representative of the domestic bourgeoisie, but he also helps keep open the terrain of compromise with certain sectors of the comprador bourgeoisie, as is shown by the arrangements made with the United States on the occasion of his visit to Washington. The AFM itself, however, is very divided, underneath the carefully cultivated illusion of a unanimous facade. As we shall see, it broadly represents a very particular alliance between the domestic bourgeoisie and the radicalized petty bourgeoisie, with even an alliance within its own ranks between the Higher Council of the AFM (the 'Council of 20') and the Co-ordinating Committee, which is far more radicalized.

Nor is the domestic bourgeoisie absent from the political parties represented in the present Portuguese government. To take the Socialist Party first of all, the most significant wing of the party, that led by Mario Soares, who dominated its congress of December 1974, is very dependent on the German SPD, and leans strongly towards a right social-democratic policy of the Willy Brandt variety; this provoked a split in the Socialists' ranks and the departure of its radicalized wing under Manuel Serra. Above all, however, the domestic bourgeoisie is represented at the party level by the PPD (Popular Democratic Party) of Sà Carneiro, 'centre-left' in the style of the former MRP in France, with a vaguely 'radical-socialist' veneer – the party particularly cultivated by Washington. Alongside the Socialist Party, this party represents the effective political restructuring of the bourgeoisie on the basis of the new compromise between the domestic and the comprador bourgeoisie, firmly supported by the Confederation of Portuguese Industrialists which we have mentioned previously, and by the 'enlightened' wing of the Catholic Church.

These various elements, taken together, seem to indicate that the Portuguese process of democratization, which will probably follow an electoral path sooner or later, is not embarked on a genuine anti-monopoly policy of the type of the French Common Programme. It should be understood here that I am talking of the present situation, and that such a policy is still completely possible in the future, being bound up with a possible 'institutionalization' of the role of the AFM in Portuguese political life, as well as other factors.

On the other hand, however, given the extremely concentrated character of the Portuguese economy, and the almost total absence of a public sector, limited measures of nationalization are probable, even in the immediate future, though these are more likely to resemble the process that took place in France and Italy after the Second World War, than the implementation of a genuine anti-monopoly programme. Finally, given the structures of landed property and agriculture in Portugal, measures of agrarian reform are even more probable in the short term, as these are indispensable for capitalism itself; this is in fact by far the most important aspect of the February 1975 economic programme.

To come back to the fundamental question. For all that has

taken place in Portugal, there has certainly not been up till now, in the overthrow of the dictatorship, any telescoping together of the process of democratization with a process of transition to socialism and of national liberation. Furthermore, even the consolidation of the democratization process itself will require further considerable transformations and purges in the state apparatuses, and particularly in the army. Besides the absence of an anti-monopoly alliance, it is this element above all that makes for the similarity between Portugal and Greece. The differences between the concrete modalities of this process should of course not be neglected. It is certainly not right to see Karamanlis as a 'successful Spinola', if only on account of the absence of a *colonialist* comprador bourgeoisie in Greece of the same type as the Portuguese, the greater strength of the domestic bourgeoisie in Greece compared with Portugal, the Greek withdrawal from the NATO military organization (Portugal remaining within this), and finally the fact that the Karamanlis government helped defeat the coup d'état of February 1975, attempted by those nostalgic for the dictatorship. It is none the less the case that what we see in Greece is a 'right-wing' sequel to the military dictatorship, and in Portugal a 'left-wing' one. But once one gets beyond the level of political representation, poses the basic questions and seeks the class basis of these processes, the difference between the two consists at the present time chiefly in the positions of strength that the popular masses and their organizations have managed to obtain in Portugal, *for their future struggles* – history does not stop short with the process of democratization.

One thing is certain, at all events. What has been proved in these countries, or is in the course of being proved, is that the overthrow of the dictatorships is possible even without the process of democratization being telescoped together with a process of transition to socialism and national liberation; furthermore, that this is possible, at least during an initial period, under the hegemony of the domestic bourgeoisie. This fact was far from evident to all who were involved in the resistance; we most often considered that this bourgeoisie was unable to have such a place, to play this role in a genuine break with the regime and the replacement of one form of state (dictatorship) by another (bourgeois 'democracy') – a decisive difference, even within the bourgeois state. This indicates that the domestic bourgeoisie has often been doubly underestimated: not just as a possible ally, but also, and this matters far more here, as an adversary, for even if experience shows that it can be an ally in certain particular conjunctures, it does not cease to be at the same time an adversary. It is obvious that democratization is far more radical, even without a telescoping of the 'democratic stage' with the 'socialist stage', when it is conducted under the hegemony and effective leadership of the working class, in a protracted and uninterrupted process of stages. To put it another way, the forms of 'democratic' regime that replace the dictatorships run the risk of remaining compromised, for a long period, by the way in which these regimes have been overthrown. At the present time, this compromise still weighs heavy on the workers' movement. If the overthrow of the dictatorships is or will be a considerable gain for the workers' movement, in the longer term, we should not pretend that it is not also at the same time a victory for the domestic bourgeoisie, which has in some respects come out of it temporarily strengthened. It is this situation that contributes to the characteristic instability of the democratization process in the countries in question.

IV

The Popular Classes

We come now to the position and attitude of the popular masses under these regimes.

In this connection, too, the effects of the new form of dependence of these countries towards imperialism, and the industrialization that results from it, made themselves felt: spectacular increase and concentration of the urban working class, depopulation and exodus from the countryside, proletarianization of a section of the peasantry, massive increase in the non-productive workers composing the new middle class (various categories of white-collar employees, technicians, officials, etc.), as also in the liberal professions, stagnation or decline of the handicraft, manufacturing and commercial petty bourgeoisie.

Together with these changes has gone a rise in class struggles. This is quite understandable, once we take account of the particular problems created by structural changes in the context of a dependent economy, and the dis-articulation of social relations provoked by an 'externally centred' industrialization process, one governed by the movement of foreign capital. Its particular effect is an endemically high rate of unemployment, open or camouflaged, which is not just due to the need for an industrial reserve army, but also to the particularly uneven development between industry and agriculture that characterizes capitalist development in the dominated countries. In agriculture, whether 'pre-capitalist' relations have been dissolved on a massive scale, or as in some cases 'preserved', the result is in both cases their dis-articulation by the accelerated penetration and reproduction of capitalism. (In the Greek case, the extreme parcellization of small peasant ownership.)

These tendencies all contribute to releasing unoccupied labour-power which gravitates towards the towns, where the particular characteristics of the industrialization process fail to provide it with corresponding jobs. This imbalance in employment, and the similarly characteristic lack of adaptation to the labour market, give rise to several forms of unemployment: the unemployment of an immense 'suburban' population concentrated in shanty towns around the urban centres, living from hand to mouth or off various services; unemployment of a significant intellectual sub-proletariat of peasant children making their way through the educational apparatus in order to find jobs in the 'tertiary' sector, and in public and semi-public administration, while eking out an existence by means of part-time and illegal work, etc. (characteristic hypertrophy of the urban sector in Portugal, Spain and Greece). This phenomenon is sometimes described as 'marginality', but this is doubly incorrect; in the first place, it is a structural feature of dependent capitalism, while on the other hand, these masses play an important political role. It is also the corollary of emigration, particularly in the Portuguese and Greek cases.

The above needs a little explanation. It is not in fact endogenous unemployment that is the cause of emigration, as is often said, but if anything the reverse. It follows from the uneven development of various countries under imperialism that the internationalization of capital and production always involves a dual movement: export of capital from the imperialist countries to the dependent countries, and export of labour-power from the dependent countries to the imperialist countries, the capital of these latter exploiting labour-power both where it is originally found and within its own home territory. There are many reasons why immigrant labour is absolutely indispensable for the capital of the dominant countries. In the present phase of imperialism, in particular, the main counteracting tendency to the falling rate of profit lies in the intensive exploitation of labour. This gives rise both to new forms of export of capital to the dependent countries (dependent industrialization), and to the dual tendency of over-qualification/dis-qualification of labour that accompanies the rise in labour productivity (relative surplus-value) within the imperialist countries themselves. The dis-qualification of labour within the imperialist countries is one reason among others which makes the presence and super-exploitation of unskilled immigrant workers indispensable. On the other hand, however, it is the dependent industrialization of the dominated countries which makes the labour-power of these countries available for emigration, by the dis-articulation of their social relationships that it involves. In Greece, Portugal and Spain, this emigration is precisely an accompaniment of their 'development'.

It is this structural necessity of emigration that accompanies the reproduction of the dominant capital in the dominated countries, which is at the root of the unemployment there (more strictly speaking, the transitional lack of employment); there is no need to see in this any Machiavellian machinations of the imperialist bourgeoisies, simply objective tendencies of capital accumulation in the present phase of imperialism. If I stress this particular phenomenon, it is because of its effects on the social struggles in these countries, effects that cut two ways: this emigration has undoubtedly helped to promote the struggles of those who see themselves forced to leave their own country in order to provide for their families, but it has also functioned, right up to recent years, as a safety-valve in the face of such struggles.

We shall just mention some particular forms of these struggles. First of all, the many struggles of the working class, which is always in the vanguard of popular struggles. In the first instance, these are struggles for particular demands, concerning wages and job security, not always expressed in the form of open strikes, given the repression exercized by the dictatorships, but also in more subtle forms of working-class resistance that are just as formidable for the bosses – absenteeism, low productivity, disorganization of the labour process (the famous southern 'laziness'). Original forms of struggle have also sprung up around these objectives that also appear in other European countries in the present imperialist conjuncture: struggles by the suburban population already mentioned, but above all struggles by the mass of workers penned into the large production units. We can list: (i) struggles against the conditions of work and against the forms of increase in labour productivity imposed by the multi-national corporations (relative surplus-value) on workers fresh from the land; (ii) struggles for health, and over social facilities, the base of these being the development of the new urban middle class; (iii) peasant struggles against the pro-letarianization of the countryside, against the growth of the gap (the 'scissors') between the price of industrial products and that of agricultural products, which is a characteristic feature of this phase of industrialization, and also against the expropriation of agricultural land for the building of new factories; (iv) the rise of women's liberation struggles, given their involvement in economic activity in the non-productive sector; (v) the prodigious development of student struggles, deriving among other things from the characteristic gap between the labour market and the educational apparatus, which is involved in redistributing agents between the countryside and urban wage labour, but which in fact opens onto an endemic unemployment; (vi) finally, the consider-able rise in the struggles of intellectuals, in the broad sense, characteristic of countries where the bourgeoisie is weak and thus unable to establish a clear ideological hegemony and cement 'organic' ties with this stratum, a fact that marks the failure of the military dictatorships, as opposed to the relative success of the fascist regimes proper, on the ideological front – on the contrary, the very persistence of the dictatorship in Spain, and its establishment in Greece, helped to dissolve the ideological sequels of the civil war which kept large strata of intellectuals at a distance from the popular masses.

The fact that should particularly be stressed here is there-fore the direct participation of a considerable portion of the new urban petty bourgeoisie in these struggles over the last few years. This is something that very clearly distinguishes this class from its attitude with regard to Nazism in Germany and fascism in Italy, in the inter-war period, and even from its much more recent passivity in Portugal and Spain. (In Spain, a favourite theme of conservative papers and opinion nowadays is that of the 'subversion of the middle classes'.) This phenomenon forms part of a more general movement visible throughout the European continent, namely a tendency towards the convergence of the subjective class positions of the white-collar workers with those of the working class, a delayed result of the major transformations that the objective class situation of this stratum has undergone in the present phase. Although this convergence is not altogether free of ambiguities, and in the countries we are dealing with here it takes place essentially on the basis of nationalism – viz. the various regionalist and nationalist movements in Spain, the intense anti-Americanism in Greece – it is still the case that this nationalism has clearly taken a progressive turn in the most recent period. On the one hand, it attests to real aspirations of national independence that are crucial in the present phase of imperialism, and which break with the official reactionary nationalism of the dictatorships; on the other hand, to a clearly populist turn in the cultural and ideological protest of this new petty bourgeoisie, particularly of the intellectuals (viz. the search for the 'roots of popular culture' evident in the spectacular vogue for popular song, and the protest role it plays with these strata, from the *nova cançо* in Spain to the *rebetiko* in Greece), a way through which this new petty bourgeoisie can live its convergence with the popular masses. In any event, this petty bourgeoisie, the liberal professions and the intellectuals have been present on a massive scale in the struggles for democratic freedoms.

The upsurge in the struggles of the new petty bourgeoisie is particularly significant on account of its effects among the personnel of the state apparatuses, and the armed forces in particular. But it is necessary for all that to dwell for a moment on the ambiguity of the petty bourgeoisie's attitude. Because of the nationalist orientation of the movement, this class has been mobilized up till now predominantly under the leadership of the domestic bourgeoisie. This is still the case even when a part of the new petty bourgeoisie has been clearly radicalized in the direction of the popular masses, as is evidently the case in Portugal, but also in Greece with the movement of Andreas Papandreou. The domestic bourgeoisie has successfully exploited the new petty bourgeoisie's nationalism in its own contradictions with the comprador bourgeoisie, also putting forward those themes to which this petty bourgeoisie is particularly sensitive on account of its class position ('technocracy', 'Europeanization', 'development', 'modernization', etc.). We can say that although the tactical combination of the domestic bourgeoisie and the working class with the aim of overthrowing the dictatorships dissolved the hesitations of the petty bourgeoisie and threw it massively into the opposition, its convergence with the popular masses has been realized precisely by way of the domestic bourgeoisie – and it is in this way that it has essentially taken part in the dictatorships' overthrow. This explains among other things both the ulterior evolution of the Karamanlis government in Greece, and the present obstacles to further radicalization in Portugal.

It is not possible, within the limits of this essay, to undertake a deeper analysis of the struggles which took place under the dictatorships, nor to examine the important role played by the left in organizing them, particularly (though not exclusively) by the Communist Parties of these countries, the Spanish Communist Party above all. In the Spanish case, at least, these struggles are well known, though in Greece and Portugal, where they were less spectacular and in fact less significant, they often remained unknown to the public at large, particularly outside of the country. Besides the police repression, another element clearly had important effects both on the forms that these struggles took and on certain of their limitations at the political level, an element that was for a long time under-estimated by the resistance organizations. Although the phase of dependent industrialization involves a considerably increased exploitation of the popular masses, yet as far as the urban masses are concerned, this exploitation has been mainly a relative one, at least up until recently; as we have already noted, it involved a growing gap between the rise in wages on the one hand, and the increase in profits and in labour productivity on the other. This increased exploitation was not of an absolute kind, and in fact the real purchasing power of the urban masses even increased during this phase and under the dictatorship regimes. This is true for all classes and strata involved, if to an unequal extent.

According to OECD statistics, the average annual rises in hourly wage rates and consumer prices, between 1966 and 1971, were, for Greece, 8.8 per cent and 2.1 per cent respectively, for Spain, 12.3 per cent and 5.4 per cent, and for Portugal, 10.2 per cent and 7.8 per cent. Although there is a lack of more detailed statistics for the various classes and strata (working class, white-collar employees, various categories of managers and executives), the increase in purchasing power is very clear in the cases of Spain and Greece, if somewhat less so in Portugal (where wages are still among the lowest in Europe, i.e. wretched). Another indication of this, though in this case a very rough one, is the increase in the average per capita national income, in Spain and Greece in particular. In 1964, this was 500 dollars per head in Spain and 590 dollars in Greece, while the Greek figure has now passed the 1500 dollar mark, with Spain also approaching this. On the other hand, the gap between wages, and the level of profits and labour productivity, has considerably increased. In Greece, profits rose at an annual rate of 13 per cent between 1967 and 1969, while in Spain, the annual increase in labour productivity was 7 per cent between 1964 and 1966, and that of real wages 4.6 per cent.

In speaking of an actual increase in purchasing power of this kind, it is necessary to bear in mind the particular place that these countries occupy in the dependent zone, and also of course the very low real income that they had to start with. But if the dictatorships are in no way responsible for this improvement, the fact remains that they were not able to prevent it, in the face of the resistance movements and the class struggle. This is manifestly the case in Greece, where the improvement began in the 1960s, well before the colonels' regime, and continued under it. And it is certainly a factor making for a certain limitation in the political development of these struggles.

But this increase in real purchasing power is only compatible for a certain period with the structures of dependence characteristic of the present phase, and the rapid accumulation of foreign capital in these countries; it also exhibits substantial variations and oscillations. Given the contradictions of capitalist accumulation at the international level, these countries become the weak links in any crisis of capitalist accumulation, the dominant imperialist countries expelling and exporting in their direction the initial effects of the crisis (inflation, unemployment, etc.). This is particularly clear in the present capitalist crisis – and on a quite different level, it is also true for the present relations between the United States and Europe. The organic position of these countries in the global process of monopoly capitalist accumulation, and the induced reproduction of foreign capital within them, is what makes possible this direct export of the effects of the crisis (for instance, the role of the multinationals in the present inflation). Given the particular inability of the dictatorships, narrowly linked as they are to the dominant foreign capital, to take even the minimum 'national' measures required to confront this crisis, it struck the working classes of these countries, and the urban masses in general, with all its force. A simple example of this is that these countries, and Portugal and Greece in particular, beat all European records for inflation in the course of the last two years (25 per cent in Portugal and 30 per cent in Greece, for the year 1973 and the beginning of 1974).

The former improvement in purchasing power was thus only to be matched by a sharp and spectacular fall in the recent period of capitalist crisis, a fall accompanied by an increase in unemployment, and intensified by the restrictions imposed by the dominant countries on the flow of immigration that the bourgeoisies there had themselves created. It is quite remarkable, moreover, how the effects of the crisis here preceded its effects in the other European countries, and were felt prior to the overthrow of the dictatorships in Portugal and Greece; this was one way in which the capital of the dominant countries was able to delay the effects of the crisis in its home territory.

At all events, this crisis played a role of its own in the over-throw of the Portuguese and Greek regimes, and in the process under way in Spain already before Franco's death; the removal of the brake imposed by the improvement in living standards opened the way to an upsurge of mass struggles.

Since the crisis had its effects in this way, rather than being directly determinant, we must come back to the particular features of the mass struggles. These were in no way limited simply to economic demands. On the one hand, the very form of the dictatorship regime meant that any economic struggle, which in most cases was illegal (abolition of the right to strike, in one form or another), assumed a clear political aspect; by its very existence, it was an act of resistance against the regime. On the other hand, there was also a definite and open political struggle by the popular classes, either in illegal forms, or by exploiting the possibilities of legal or semi-legal forms of struggle that spaces within the regime made possible. What was lacking, however, both before and during the crisis, was a mass movement developing in 'frontal' attacks or assault waves which could defeat the regime directly, whether in the form of people's war, or that of movements culminating in a political general strike, or alternatively in that of a general insurrectionary uprising. I do not mean by this simply the absence of a precisely located attack such as the 'storming of the Winter Palace'; what is at issue here is not just the absence of a precise insurrectionary moment of this kind, which would greatly simplify the problem. The point is that there was not under these regimes the kind of 'protracted process' through which a massive popular movement can develop towards a frontal attack against the state.

There are two apparent exceptions to this.

Firstly, the Polytechnic uprising in Athens. This was an

unprecedented movement in the annals of the twentieth century fascist regimes and dictatorships in Europe. Some 300,000 people took part in it, the students being joined by large numbers of workers (particularly those in building and marine construction, the spearhead of the Greek workers' movement), peasants (the peasants of Attica protesting against the expropriation of land), new middle class elements and intellectuals, who all confronted the junta's tanks. The number of dead is known only as somewhere between 50 and 100, and there were hundreds severely wounded. But although the Polytechnic uprising in some respects sounded the death-knell of the Greek dictatorship, it in no way succeeded in directly overthrowing it, and remained relatively isolated in the country as a whole.

There is also the case for Portugal of the African national liberation movements in the Portuguese colonies, which there is an unfortunate tendency often to forget. In the present phase of internationalization of capital and production, nothing could be more stupid than to ignore the role that these movements played in the actual overthrow of the Caetano regime. And this is paralleled in some respects also by the armed popular resistance of the Cypriot people to the coup d'état unleashed by the Greek junta and its local supporters, the EOKA-B, against Makarios. It is amazing how the role of 'international events' is brought up in connection with the overthrow of these regimes, while quietly forgetting to say that these were in the last analysis nothing less than popular uprisings against these regimes by their vassals.

Yet even here, the role of these struggles was not a direct one; if it was not just a matter of 'external' factors, their impact was still felt chiefly 'at a distance', above all in intensifying the contradictions within the dictatorships themselves, and particularly in their main pillar, the armed forces. Strictly speaking, these struggles were articulated to the contradictions of the national social formations in Portugal and Greece, helping to condense these, and thus marking the beginning of the downfall of regimes in both cases already well undermined from within. The effect of these struggles must also not be overestimated, and this is particularly important as regards the Spanish case: to believe that nothing will happen in Spain in the absence of factors of this kind would be as wrong as to directly attribute the fall of the Portuguese and Greek dictatorships to the colonial war in Africa and the Greek colonels' adventure in Cyprus. After all, there have been very many examples of successful national liberation struggles that did not have direct effects on the internal regimes of the colonial powers. The national liberation struggles in Africa, and the friction between the people of Cyprus and the Athens regime, had both lasted a very long time before they came to latch onto the particular contradictions within the Portuguese and Greek armies. We repeat, then, that except in the case of direct invasion (Nazi Germany and fascist Italy), it has always been the internal contradictions of a given country that have so far played the predominant role in fundamental changes in its forms of state and regime. The national liberation struggles, just like American imperialism from the other side, only influenced these countries to the extent that their effects were internalized within them.

There was no frontal mass movement against the dictatorships, and in this sense, the popular struggles were not the direct or principal factor in their overthrow. Nevertheless, these struggles were certainly the determining factor. What I mean by this is that the factors directly involved in this overthrow (the regimes' own internal contradictions) were themselves determined by the popular struggles. This already indicates the site and the complexity of the basic problem: in what way, exactly, did these popular struggles (the determining factor) produce the effects (the principal factor) that directly contributed to the overthrow of the dictatorships? We are familiar enough with the reply of the bourgeoisie: basing itself on the undeniable fact that the overthrow was not directly brought about by a popular mass movement, it maintains that the popular struggles counted for nothing in this process, or at least for very little.

This point is the first to bear in mind here. But a second

must also be noted, which I shall come back to in the next chapter. The popular masses did not just play the role of determining the internal contradictions that directly contributed to the downfall of the dictatorships, but another role as well. Although the regimes' internal contradictions governed the decisive beginnings of the process, the fact that this was still a genuine process of democratization meant that in both Greece and in Portugal, the popular masses intervened by way of bitter struggles. Nothing would be more wrong than to see the overthrow of the dictatorships as having been fully achieved in Portugal on 25th April, with the accession of Spinola to power, or in Greece on 23rd July, with the return of Karamanlis. In other words, the regimes' internal contradictions, which were themselves the effects of the mass struggles, also functioned as the occasion for a direct intervention by the masses, once the process of democratization got under way.

As far as the first point is concerned, the popular and political opposition to the dictatorships found expression in a quite particular way, the importance of which we must now examine, namely in the characteristic disaffection of the masses towards these regimes, leading to their isolation from the masses – to a different extent in each case. This was the situation in Greece right from the start, or at least very soon after; in Portugal, as also in Spain, it took place gradually, as the regimes there had originally enjoyed a certain popular support, particularly in the countryside. In the last few years, this mute, varied, but constant resistance by the people to the dictatorships was a feature distinguishing them from the classical fascist regimes, although, as is the case with every concrete exceptional regime, these dictatorships themselves were each a unique combination of various regimes of the exceptional state; they did in fact display certain fascist elements, but always under the dominant form of military dictatorship. In point of fact, the regimes in these countries either never succeeded in implanting themselves in the masses, or they gradually lost whatever popular base they had enjoyed; either they never managed to set up their own organizations of mass mobilization and indoctrination, a fascist party or relatively 'representative' unions, (in the Greek case, despite repeated attempts in this direction by the junta), or if they did, these organizations ended up as no more than ossified relics (as with the Falange and the Movimiento Nacional in Spain).

The isolation of these dictatorships, and their difference in this respect from the fascist regimes proper, is of the greatest importance. It has often been underestimated by the left and its organizations, and seen as simply a 'passive' resistance by the people, ultimately quite ineffective, but this is a completely false assessment. It has also led people to think of these states as separate from the 'civil society' of the popular masses, monolithically maintaining themselves in an ivory tower until a final confrontation makes them collapse like a house of cards. This isolation is thus seen as somehow preventing class contradictions from affecting the state apparatus, hardening it against internal contradictions, so that class contradictions can only be 'external' to this apparatus, i.e. located between it and the masses 'outside' the state. In such a conception, the internal contradictions of these apparatuses would be no more than the friction between clans and camarillas above or outside of class contradictions.

This conception, of course, has proved itself false. What is more, it makes it impossible to grasp a seemingly paradoxical feature of the military dictatorships. For if the enlistment of the popular classes in the fascist apparatuses, and in certain cases, particularly that of the petty bourgeoisie, its voluntary enrolment in them, created considerable internal contradictions within the Nazi and Italian fascist apparatuses (parties/states), reflecting the direct contradictions within them between the interests of these classes and those of big capital, these contradictions have been far more pronounced in the case of the military dictatorships, despite their 'isolation' from the popular classes, in a situation where the classes have not been directly and massively present and mobilized in this way. Furthermore, these contradictions have played a far more important role in the fall of the military dictatorships than they did in the overthrow of the fascist regimes proper.

The question then arises as to how the contradictions between the dominant and dominated classes could affect a state apparatus particularly 'isolated' from them. In other words, how did the weight of the popular masses make itself felt within state apparatuses from which these masses were apparently absent (either because they were excluded, or because they simply kept themselves aloof)?

To answer this question, a brief theoretical detour is necessary. The relationship between the state and social classes has most often been viewed as one of externality; this is a typical feature of bourgeois ideology, but it has also had its effects on the Marxist theory of the state. In this problematic, the state is considered either as a *subject* or as a *thing*. Considered as a subject, we are back at the old Hegelian conception of a state that really is 'separate' from 'civil society', endowed with an intrinsic rationality as the embodiment of the general will in the face of atomized individuals. This conception is directly reflected in the work of the young Marx, and it still persists in his later statements on the state as an 'organism independent of society and above it', i.e. a characteristic parallel to the state's function of class domination. Viewed as a thing, we have the 'instrumentalist' conception also present within Marxism; the state is considered as by its nature a mere instrument, a machine, that can be manipulated at will by the dominant classes, and whose relationship of representation with their class interests is supposedly due to their 'grip' on this inert instrument. The political repercussions of these two positions, which are each as false as the other, are incalculable, but there is one such effect, common to both of them, that is particularly important for us here; in this problematic of the state/classes relationship (or that of state/social groups-civil society) as one of two separate entities confronting one another, classes are seen as acting on the state only from outside, by the play of 'influences', each of them taking hold of a piece of the state, or the state as a whole. In this conception, the military dictatorships, in their isolation, appear as the extreme example of this instrumentality of the state.

But this precisely makes it impossible to grasp the internal contradictions of the state itself. In no case, in fact, is the state a subject or a thing; it is always by nature a relation, just as is 'capital': to be more precise, the condensation of the balance of forces between the classes that is expressed in a specific manner within the state. Just as 'capital' already contains in itself the contradiction between capital and wage-labour, so class contradictions always cut right through the state, because the state reproduces these class contradictions within itself by its very nature as a class state. This means in effect that class contradictions are always expressed, in a specific way, as internal contradictions within the state, which never is and can never be a monolithic bloc devoid of fissures. There is certainly always a unity of state power related to the state's representation of the interests of the hegemonic class or fraction, and this is the reason why the popular classes can never occupy the state apparatus bit by bit, but have to smash it in the transition to socialism; but this should not give rise to the idea of the state as a bloc devoid of fissures.

To return to the military dictatorships that we are concerned with here. Just as with every bourgeois state, their relationship to the popular classes is expressed in internal contradictions involving the various political and economic measures they have to take towards them, i.e. the particular modalities of capital accumulation. In actual fact, the contradictions between the various fractions of the bourgeoisie themselves always express, in the last analysis, different tactics and modalities for the exploitation and domination of the popular masses. This is to do no more than formulate, in class terms, the fact that the contradictions of capitalist accumulation are ultimately due to the class struggle, and the fact that the very cycle of capitalist reproduction already bears within it the contradiction between capital and the exploited classes. The various apparatuses of these military dictatorships, and their leading political personnel, are subject to very serious internal shocks, of which one can give many examples; and these can only be appreciated at their true significance if behind this or that measure or policy in favour of this or that fraction of capital, we see clearly the spectre of the struggle of the popular masses.

Still more is involved. We know that the state can never exercize its function of domination, in the long run, by repression alone; this must always be accompanied by ideological domination. In the bourgeois states in general, there are even apparatuses specially designed for the politico-ideological domination of the working class and the popular masses, at least in so far as these apparatuses manage to implant themselves on a massive scale. This is particularly the case, in the parliamentary-democratic forms of the bourgeois state, with the parties and trade-unions of class collaboration (the majority of social-democratic organizations). But the same principle is at work, though in different forms, in certain regimes of the exceptional state, particularly the fascist regimes and the various kinds of right-wing populism. The enlistment and mobilization of the masses in the fascist or populist apparatuses certainly gives rise to very serious internal contradictions within these regimes, dominated as they are by big capital, and of quite a different order to those of the parliamentary-democratic regimes. The very nature of fascist regimes (their monopolization of political apparatuses) means that the contradictions between the popular classes, particularly the working class, and the bourgeoisie, are not dispersed into contradictions between various specialized apparatuses, but are actually concentrated within the 'single' political apparatus. Even so, this political apparatus, by mobilizing the masses, still enables a certain type of regulation of the contradictions within it, which does not just degenerate into a settling of accounts, so that the very existence of the regime is at stake. This makes it possible for a political line to be arrived at that has at least a minimal coherence, and which the state apparatuses are then entrusted with reflecting and applying.

But there is nothing of this kind in the state apparatuses we are dealing with here. The popular masses are nowhere to be found, though this only means, taking into account what we have just explained, that they are in fact *everywhere*. In the long run, these regimes have no powers of regulation; faced as they are with an omnipresent class enemy, unable to grasp it or predict its behaviour, let alone recuperate it, various contradictory tactics designed to neutralize it and protect themselves from it mount one on top of the other, thus contributing to a characteristic intensification of the state's internal contradictions. In point of fact, this situation leads these regimes into an amazingly incoherent muddle of policies (economic, repressive, ideological) towards the popular classes, and in the long run this incoherence actually degenerates into open conflicts among their leading circles over the tactics to adopt towards the masses, whose weight makes itself heavily felt. A particularly clear example of this is the conflict between Papadopoulos and General Ioannidis, before and during the Markezinis interlude (July–November 1973); this conflict ended with the elimination of Papadopoulos by an actual coup d'état within the coup d'état regime. The various turns made by the Franco regime in the face of its internal contradictions are also clearly visible. Ultimately, in this explosive conjuncture, it often comes about that certain leading circles, more far-seeing than others who literally lose their heads for lack of any grip on the masses, gradually come round to an 'intelligent' attitude: either a 'controlled' overthrow of the regime (Spinola, the Greek generals of the Northern army), or the toleration of a legal democratic movement not integrated into the regime (Diez Allegria, former chief of staff of the Spanish army), following in this respect the change in the policy of the domestic bourgeoisie towards the popular masses.

So far we have spoken only of the leading circles of these state apparatuses. But the rest of the hierarchy below them should not be ignored: the first lines of 'contact' with the popular masses, whether in the army, the judiciary, or the civil administration, are the intermediate and lower levels. Not only is the class origin of these strata often different from that of the top echelons (generally petty-bourgeois in Portugal and Spain, peasant and petty-bourgeois in Greece), but more importantly, they currently belong to the petty bourgeoisie (which distinguishes them from the rapidly 'bourgeoisified' leaders).

In regimes of the fascist type, not only are these intermediate and lower levels themselves strongly mobilized and united by the fascist politico-ideological structure, but they are also in contact with the masses, who participate to some extent in the organizational apparatus. There is however nothing of this kind either in the case of our military dictatorships; the middle and lower levels of the hierarchy are thus ultimately squeezed between the popular masses and the leaders, being directly affected by the class struggle and caught up in it. This accentuates the class divisions that separate these lower ranks from the top of the state apparatus, and gives rise to very strong internal contradictions between the lower and intermediate levels and the top, the most typical case of this being that of the Armed Forces Movement in Portugal. It is also necessary here to distinguish between the various different popular classes. While the struggle of the working class only produces its effects on these strata 'at a distance', that of the petty bourgeoisie affects them in a far more direct way, as we shall see.

One lesson that we can already draw from this analysis is that the struggle of the popular masses, even when it does not take the form of a general and frontal uprising against the dictatorships, has always played a determining role in their overthrow, in the last analysis; for in its initial form it already intervenes in the internal contradictions of these regimes themselves, at the point when these contradictions set under way the process of their downfall.

A second element here is that physical integration into the apparatuses so as to subvert them 'from within' is not the only means by which the popular masses can intensify the dictatorships' internal contradictions and even find allies within them; a practice of this kind would imply a quite false interpretation of the terms 'inside' and 'outside', as applied to the relationship between the popular masses and the state. It is false to draw any strategic conclusion of 'subversion from within' from the fact that these internal contradictions, and not just frontal attack, are also able to bring about the overthrow of the dictatorship regimes. The intensification of internal contradictions is never more pronounced than when the popular masses keep up a permanent struggle at a distance from the state apparatuses, and try to draw toward them the 'vacillating' elements within these apparatuses. This is precisely the case in which the effects of the mass struggle are best internalized in the very heart of the regime.

This enables us to raise a further question. If it is clear that the popular masses should at all events struggle at a distance from the state apparatuses, should they *also* integrate into them, at the same time, so as to conduct a parallel process of 'subversion from within'?

We can say right away that this question only partly coincides with the problem of 'legal' and 'illegal' struggle. There can well be, even under regimes of this kind, legal or semi-legal forms of struggle that do not involve direct participation in the organizational apparatuses: petitions of various kinds, different forms of strikes, work in the press or publishing, setting up of parallel and semi-legal organizations, workers' commissions (as in Spain) or cultural organizations (Greece). A positive response to the question of the use of certain legal forms of struggle in no way necessarily implies a positive response to the question of the presence of resistance elements in the state apparatuses.

This is already a very old question, raised by Dimitrov at the Seventh Congress of the Comintern in 1935 with respect to the fascist regimes (Dimitrov answering in the affirmative), and it has been especially important for the Greek, Spanish and Portuguese resistance, particularly with a view to deciding on the attitude to take up towards the official trade unions in these countries.

On this particular subject, there cannot be a straightforward answer one way or the other, which would hold good in all cases, for all apparatuses, and in all conjunctures. On the one hand, the popular masses and the resistance movement can take advantage of the internal contradictions of these apparatuses without having to take part in them physically; on the other hand, given these internal contradictions in the dictatorships, which – we repeat – are far from being monolithic blocs devoid of fissures, a parallel presence of the masses and of resistance elements in their apparatuses may be a way of strengthening the struggle and affecting the development of these contradictions. The strategic advantages of this may far outweigh the risks, which are real, of lending legitimacy to the apparatuses involved. The Portuguese Communist Party, in particular, succeeded quite spectacularly in practically taking over the official unions, which considerably aided the struggle of the working class in the process of overthrowing the regime. The resistance movement has to follow a narrow path between boycott (the line that predominated in the Greek resistance), and direct physical presence in these apparatuses.

To come back to the principal question: experience has proved that the overthrow of these regimes, i.e. a genuine democratic 'break' and their replacement by bourgeois but 'democratic' regimes rather than a simple change of facade (a mere normalization), is also possible by other ways than that of a massive, general and frontal insurrection by the popular classes. However, this form or path of change was far from appearing possible in advance to everyone involved in the left-wing organizations. Even among those who accepted that the overthrow of these regimes would involve a specific 'democratic stage' (and not everyone was of this opinion by any means), there were many who thought that, by the very nature of the regime, this democratic break was impossible without an insurrectionary uprising. If it was possible otherwise, this is because, apart from the elements already noted, the domestic bourgeoisie, broadly supported by the petty bourgeoisie, has managed to maintain its hegemony over the process, at least up till now. To repeat again, we cannot ignore the fact that this particular route still has and will continue to have significant effects on the forms of regime that have replaced the military dictatorships, or are about to do so in Spain.

These effects involve above all certain limits that are imposed on the democratization process, and on the purging of the state bequeathed by the military dictatorships. In particular, these limits largely derive from the fact that the popular masses, though they have intervened decisively in the process, have done so only after this was set under way 'from above', as it were, in other words when compromises between the different forces party to the regime's internal contradictions had already crystallized within the apparatuses, thus creating the 'opportunities' for their overthrow. It is possible for the popular masses to press back these limits, but they will only be able to get rid of them with difficulty, and only in the long run, since their direct intervention, while certainly not after the event – for what is involved here is a process – was none the less relatively delayed. In particular, these limits create constant difficulties for the purging and democratization of the state apparatuses from below.

In Portugal, for instance, the AFM itself, because of its internal divisions, among other things, and the balance of forces between it and a military apparatus that is as yet far from being radically purged, has often intervened, by way of the military coordination force that it created under the Second Provisional Government, after the fall of prime minister Palma Carlos (COPCON, under the command of General Carvalho), to enforce respect for the limits imposed on any *saneamento* from below – in the conflicts at the *Jornal de Comercio*, in the firm of LISNAVE, as well as those in various administrative bodies (the post office, for example). In all these conflicts, the masses demanded the dismissal of leading officials compromised by their actions under the dictatorship – though in this respect, the AFM is certainly still in the process of development.

In Greece, the position is still more clear, as far as the limits imposed on the purging of the apparatuses from below are concerned, even where the masses at the base are politically most active (the university and trade-union apparatuses for example). In the university apparatus in particular, this has already provoked explosive situations.

In both cases, then, if to a different extent, there is on the one hand a challenge by the sectors that directly set under way the overthrow of the dictatorship in the face of the initiatives from below for a purging of the state apparatuses, even though this would not go beyond the framework of 'democratization' (there have nowhere been any real attempts, in these initiatives, to set up 'soviets'); on the other hand, the masses come up against obstacles in their attempt to intervene in the 'democratization' process in an autonomous manner, i.e. otherwise than simply as the support of a purging process still directly controlled from above.

The basic problem that is still not resolved is raised here once again: even if we accept that the overthrow of these regimes is at all events a considerable victory for the popular masses, the fact that the particular path this took proved successful in no way proves that a quite different path more favourable to the popular masses would have been impossible. This decisive question is still at the heart of all debates in the left-wing organizations of these countries. In the Preface to this book I made it clear that I could not undertake to examine these organizations here, for this would require a whole book to itself. It involves both the objective coordinates, at the global level and those specific to the countries in question, as well as the strategy of the left-wing organizations, in the first place that of the Communist Parties, which were the spearhead of resistance to the dictatorships (the meaning of a 'democratic stage' in a protracted and uninterrupted process of stages towards socialism; alliances with fractions of the bourgeoisie and hegemony in these alliances; the forms of struggle, etc.).

V

The State Apparatuses

Examination of the state apparatuses of these regimes of military dictatorship provides the opportunity to go more deeply into the question of their internal contradictions.

The first basic point, already frequently mentioned, is that experience has shown, or is in the course of showing in Spain, that these dictatorships are incapable of reforming themselves, i.e. of a continuous and linear evolution towards a 'parliamentary-democratic' form of regime which would replace its predecessor by way of a controlled 'succession'. The problem here is the same, in inverse form, as that which I dealt with elsewhere as the 'rise of fascism'; just as an exceptional form of state (fascism, dictatorship, bonapartism) cannot develop out of a parliamentary-democratic state by a continuous and linear route, imperceptibly as it were, by successive steps, so a parliamentary-democratic state cannot develop in this way out of a form of exceptional state.

To understand this, it is necessary to take into due account, and not underestimate, the decisive differences that there are between these forms of the bourgeois state, both as concerns their actual structure, and the balance of forces between the classes to which they correspond. The two cases involve a different balance of forces between the dominated classes and the power bloc, and a profoundly modified balance of forces between the various components and class fractions of this power bloc itself. This is why transitions from one of these forms of state to another coincide with political crises, conjunctures in which contradictions are condensed together and punctuate the rhythm of development of the class struggle. In other words, the transition to socialism is not the only occasion for political crises leading to revolutionary situations. And even changes in the balance of forces that do not reach this level of upheaval may be associated with political crises giving rise to substantial modifications in the bourgeois state.

These crises, moreover, do not just mark the transition from a parliamentary-democratic form of state to a form of the exceptional bourgeois state; they can also mark the transition between various forms of parliamentary-democratic state (e.g. the advent of Gaullism). But they are to be found in every case of a transition from a parliamentary-democratic form of state to an exceptional form, as well as the inverse transition from an exceptional state to a parliamentary-democratic one which concerns us here.

In point of fact, one of the functions of the parliamentary-democratic state (universal suffrage, pluralism of political parties and organizations, specific relationship between the executive and parliament, juridical regulation of the respective spheres of competence of the various state apparatuses and branches), is to permit the balance of forces within the power bloc to change without a serious upheaval in the state apparatuses; this is particularly the role of the constitution and of law. The parliamentary-democratic state, with an organizational framework for the organic circulation of hegemony among different fractions of the power bloc by way of their political representatives, or even a certain regulated separation of powers between the dominant classes and fractions, only ever manages to achieve this goal in a partial way. But this proves totally impossible in the exceptional form of state. In other words, and contrary to a fairly widespread idea (the 'weakness of the democracies' vis-à-vis the 'strength of totalitarian systems'), the political crises that afflict exceptional states are far more formidable for them than is the case with the parliamentary-democratic regimes, as the latter often have at their disposal the institutional means to cope with these.

The exceptional state comes into being in order to remedy a characteristic crisis of hegemony within the power bloc, and in this bloc's relationship with the popular masses. It corresponds to a significant shift in the balance of forces. This shift or consolidation of hegemony (in Spain and Portugal towards the oligarchy: comprador capital/big landowners; in Greece in favour of comprador capital) occurs by way of a series of particular modifications which precisely congeal, at the very heart of the state, the balance of forces to which it originally corresponded. This balance of forces can only be institutionalized by way of far-reaching changes in the state apparatuses such as are characteristic of every exceptional regime: suppression of the traditional political representatives (political parties) of the fractions of the power bloc itself, elimination of the suffrage, shift of the dominant role in the state apparatuses to the repressive apparatus (in particular the armed forces), considerable strengthening of the state's 'bureaucratic' centralism, hierarchical ordering and duplication of real centres of power within the state, and of its transmission belts. All this has two results: on the one hand, a change in the balance of forces within the power bloc itself (in this case in favour of the domestic bourgeoisie) cannot come about without a radical change in this form of state, while on the other, this change cannot be effected in a linear way, by successive subtle nuances.

To understand this point better, we must take into account a factor that has not been adequately stressed up till now. The state appatatus is not a thing or a structure that is in itself neutral, so that the configuration of class power only intervenes in the form of the state power. The relations that characterize the state power also pervade the structure of its apparatus, the state being as it is the condensation of a balance of forces. It is precisely this charactetistic of the state, that it is a relation, and thus riven by class contradictions, that allots a role of their own to the state apparatuses and the agents involved in them, and enables them to play this role. This is also the basis of the fundamental Marxist thesis according to which the transition to socialism cannot take place by a simple shift in state power (the working class and its allies replacing the bourgeoisie); this transition requires the state apparatuses to be smashed, i.e. it is not just a question of replacing the heads of these apparatuses, but of a radical transformation in their actual organizational structure. What is more, the bourgeois state cannot itself give rise to a socialist state, in the event of a shift in state power to the working class (illusions of 'state socialism'), for the specific weight and role of its apparatuses is always expressed, through its own structure, as a resistance to such a transformation.

This thesis of the need to 'smash' the state apparatuses relates to the transition from capitalism to socialism. But the arguments on which it is based lose nothing of their relevance in the particular case of the transition from the exceptional bourgeois state to the parliamentary-democratic form. Of course, there is no question here of 'smashing' the state apparatuses, but it can be said, in an analogous way, that the considerable transformations that this transition to a parliamentary-democratic state require cannot be undertaken by the exceptional state itself. The specific role and weight of its institutional apparatuses imposes a massive resistance to such a transformation. This is not always the case with the transition from one form of parliamentary-democratic state to another.

In point of fact, the specific characteristics of the exceptional state are the source both of its strength and of its fragility, by virtue of their extraordinary rigidity. The slightest genuine 'opening' risks the collapse of the whole edifice. Both its skeleton and its internal cement, ideological and repressive, are based on a very delicate division between clans and factions, between branches and apparatuses that are interlocked, duplicated and hierarchically ordered to an amazing degree, in their functions and their spheres of competence. Any reorganization, even the most simple, directly affects the state as a whole, taking into account its permanent disequilibrium in the face of the class struggles that it has sought to congeal, including the struggles between classes and fractions of the power bloc itself. The internal contradictions that run through this state and its dominant apparatus (the armed forces) are a privileged form of expression for the classes deprived of their own political organizations, and they are therefore far more significant than those of a parliamentary-democratic state. The result is that these contradictions can only be controlled and contained by means of a veritable partition of the state into 'fiefs' whose relations with one another are devoid of all flexibility. This organizational feature of the exceptional state thus also leads to a specific form of relative autonomy for the various factions and clans, with each having its own power base, and certain of these, in defending their privileges, can present a permanent obstacle to possible attempts by other factions to 'normalize' the regime and help it 'evolve'.

But all this is simply one aspect of the impossibility of an internal evolution of these regimes; the most important aspect relates to the popular masses. In the extreme case, these regimes might have managed a certain degree of liberalization, as long as this only involved the power bloc in settling its own internal problems, the popular masses being excluded from this process and kept on a tight leash. This liberalization with respect to the power bloc would be an indispensable condition for the latter to set up an autonomous political organization with which to confront the popular masses, which for their part were already politically organized by the left-wing organizations in underground conditions (this was the original objective of Spanish Prime Minister Arias Navarro's 'law on associations'). But this is plainly impossible, for two reasons. Firstly, because it is to a large extent the upsurge of struggle by the popular classes that has intensified the contradictions within the power bloc, contradictions that require for their own resolution a change in the form of state, but always in the context of the relationship of each fraction within this bloc to the popular masses; at the point at which the exceptional state finds itself obliged to change in its relationship to the power bloc, there is already an upsurge of mass struggle. From this very fact, any opening of 'controlled liberalization' on the part of the state rapidly becomes a gaping hole through which the popular movement rushes in. How can the state authorize the creation of 'relatively representative' trade unions, for instance, in order to permit the power bloc to 'negotiate' with them, when this very breach in the dyke leads to the unions being rapidly occupied by the genuine representatives of the popular masses (the experience of the workers' commissions in Spain)? How can it liberalize the censorship of the press and publishing, with the aim of bringing into being a stratum of 'organic intellectuals' for the power bloc, when this liberalization can immediately be exploited by the popular masses and their own intellectuals (Greece, Spain, or even Portugal)? And how can it grant the universities certain 'freedoms' and 'corporative elections' to secure the neutrality of the intelligentsia and the youth, when these measures rapidly degenerate, as far as the dictatorships are concerned, into events on the pattern of the Polytechnic uprising in Greece?

In other words, the dictatorships are faced with the need to undertake a change at a point when they can no longer manage to control the popular movement by force, and precisely because they cannot manage to do so; this in itself means that they cannot in any way control and direct their own transformation. The regimes find themselves faced with the age-old dilemma: either they give too little, and then the changes they have in mind will in no way meet the needs of the situation; or these changes act as an incentive for more, and then the regimes appear almost automatically to have given too much.

It is in this context, the necessity and inevitability of a democratic break in the change of regime, that the events in Greece and Portugal can be understood. This break was perfectly clear in Portugal, with the alliance of the Armed Forces Movement and Spinola against the Caetano regime, which opened the way to a decisive intervention by the popular masses, the breadth and power of which is well-known. This directly provoked the fall of Spinola, the decisive turning-point in the democratization process. The break was less clear-cut in the Greek case, as it was concealed by the appearance of the army 'itself' handing back power to Karamanlis and the civilians. This appearance is of course quite misleading. In the first place, it was not a question of 'the army' as such, but of a genuine *pronunciamento* by officers of the Northern army, supported by the navy and air force, against the Athens junta. Further, it is doubtful whether things really did unfold according to the 'will' of this *pronunciamento* and the limping compromise with the junta that was its result. The statements submitted by the leading members of the junta to the examining magistrate at the time of their arrest shed a good deal of light on this. It is likely that the rebel Greek officers, just like Spinola first of all (when he was dismissed by Caetano), originally had in mind a change without any democratic break, a regime in which, while concessions were made to civilian rule, major levers of control would be left in the hands of the armed forces, and civil liberties would still be relatively controlled. This would seem to be confirmed by the abortive military putsch attempted in February 1975.

This plan also left out of account the popular forces, who waged a bitter struggle during the period following the 'fall' of the Greek junta; the game was far from over, and the process of bringing the army and police to heel (if only relatively), only got gradually under way. These struggles not only gave rise to massive and forceful demonstrations, but also and even especially, to a decisive mass intervention by the soldiers called up at the time of the general mobilization decided upon in the face of the risk of war with Turkey. This intervention took the form of a permanent battle within the different units between the officers loyal to the junta and the new recruits, including the officer recruits (who also played a very important role in Portugal). It was also struggles such as these that forced the question of the monarchy to be settled by way of a popular referendum, and contributed to the dismissal of the king as its result, an important turning-point in the democratization process. Lastly, it was the mobilization of the popular masses and their organizations that put a stop to the military putsch attempted in February 1975, an event which opened the way to a major purge in the armed forces.

All this shows the definite need for a genuine break, but also that this break actually takes the form of a 'process'. (This is again analogous, in the opposite direction, to the transition from a parliamentary-democratic state to an exceptional form). We see that the internal contradictions of the dictatorships, which are the decisive factor in setting this process under way, also provide the popular masses with opportunities to intervene in the actual realization of this break.

This role of the masses should prove still more significant in Spain, where the popular movement is far stronger than it was under the Greek and Portuguese regimes. In Spain, it may seem far less probable at the present time, for lack of the particular conditions that obtained in Greece and Portugal, that the opportunity for popular intervention will arise actually within the army itself, at least in the form that it did in those countries. These internal contradictions however, decisive as they are, are in the last analysis never more than an opportunity for the intervention of the popular masses, and they certainly do exist in Spain too. Moreover, in the context of such internal contradictions, the opportunity for popular intervention need not just come from some chance event, but can also be created by the uncontrollable skidding of a change inaugurated by a section of the regime itself, originally with quite a different motive in mind. By way of example, if I can venture on hypotheses, it can in no way be ruled out that when Franco dies or has to abandon power, the section of the military apparatus that banks on the planned succession of Juan Carlos, in the face of the 'ultras', finds that, like the Greek generals of the Northern army, it has unwittingly provided the opportunity for a democratic break. In the Spanish case, however, it is also likely that the regime's internal contradictions (which manifested themselves in February 1975 with the signing of a petition for general amnesty by some 2000 officers) will basically prevent the army, internally divided as it is, from intervening to quash the democratization process, which in this case may well be set in motion by the popular masses themselves, given the strength of the popular movement and the characteristic decay of the regime. These two forms of the democratization process may of course be combined.

To come back to the question we raised earlier. The democratic break is concretely embodied in certain major institutional changes and in significant changes in the leading personnel of the various state apparatuses: dismissals and purges. This has been the case both in Portugal and in Greece, though to differing degrees that bear on the different circumstances in which the dictatorships were overthrown. In the Greek case in particular, contrary to the impression that the protracted character of the process might produce, the army (particularly after the abortive putsch of February 1975), police and para-military bodies, as well as the judicial, educational and university apparatuses, were all purged of a quite considerable section of elements directly compromised with the colonels' junta.

It is evident for all that, however, that in both cases the conjuncture in which the overthrow of the dictatorship took place meant that these dismissals and transformations remained within the limits of a 'continuity' of the state. Not only was there not a democratic transformation of the anti-monopoly alliance type, but the democratic break also took place under the hegemony of the bourgeoisie, as we have shown in some detail in the case of Portugal. In conditions such as these, it is clear that the purging of the state apparatuses constantly comes up against limits imposed by the balance of class forces. An appreciable section of the state agents, irredeemable from the point of view of the democratic and popular movement, but certainly useful to the bourgeoisie with an eye to future struggles, remains in place, and thus in close osmosis with the bourgeoisie's own political apparatuses as these are reconstructed. This phenomenon is all the more acute in that a section of the bourgeoisie's traditional political personnel was itself guilty of complicity with the dictatorships. This was notoriously the case in Greece, for a large section of cadres in Karamanlis's old National Radical Union, from which the backbone of his new movement is largely recruited, despite a certain democratic renovation (the 'New Democratic' party). These factors also show their effects in the characteristic slowness with which the democratization of the state apparatuses proceeds, this democratization needing constant struggles on the part of the popular masses.

The limits that I mentioned earlier as limits to a 'democratization from below' are thus also found here as limits to a 'democratization from above'. They are perfectly clear in Greece, in all branches of the state, so I shall only mention here the analogous limits in Portugal, which are somewhat less familiar. First of all, while the PIDE and the Portuguese Legion were completely dismantled, two para-military formations that were basic pillars of the Salazar regime, the GNR (National Republican Guard, a force of 10,000 men) and the PSP (a specialized anti-riot police force some 14,000 strong) are still as they were, merely with certain changes in their command. Both Spinola and the new president Costa Gomes were at one time commanders of the GNR, while the PSP showed its colours by firing on the crowd besieging the rioting PIDE prisoners in August 1974, until the arrival of COPCON.

The purging of the army itself has also been clearly limited so far, as a result of the compromises reached between the AFM and the military hierarchy under Spinola and Costa Gomes. The air force, which is far from being 'progressive', and in which the AFM is very weak, is also still practically unaffected. In the course of the two months following the revolution of April 25th, some twenty-five generals were retired, but the dismissal of around 400 senior officers compromised by their role under the dictatorship, which the AFM planned after the July crisis (dismissal of Palma Carlos), could not be fully carried through, even after the eviction of Spinola. Costa Gomes' accession to the presidency was expressed in the discharging of two generals and three air-force commanders, all very senior officers. But the sum total of all these departures still left many colonels and lieutenant-colonels in their positions who were notorious supporters of Spinola, if not of the old regime, sometimes in operational commands; which means that Spinola himself is not so far off-stage as he might seem. (The AFM only includes career officers, and no more than some 400 out of a total of 4000 in the three services.) One exception in this respect is the navy, both because of the strength of the AFM here and because of the pressure from rank-and-file sailors. Shortly after April 25th, eighty-two admirals and rear-admirals were retired from the service. Finally, while the local civilian authorities have undergone a substantial purge, the extent of this has been markedly uneven. The northern agricultural provinces of the Portuguese 'interior' have been but little affected by democratization, despite the campaigns of 'cultural dynamization' undertaken by the AFM. To sum up, even the consolidation of the democratization process in Portugal still requires substantial transformation and purging of the state apparatuses and the armed forces.

The limits to democratization do not simply involve the precise paths followed by the 'democratic stage'; they also bear on the very fact of this stage itself. Just like any democratization in the context of a bourgeois state, this ultimately comes up against the hard kernel that gives all forms of the bourgeois state a certain 'continuity', i.e. a natural kinship – even if there are distinctions here related to the balance of forces. In the present phase of imperialism, these limits are quickly reached, as they are consubstantial here with the bourgeois character of the state. They are not simply imposed on the purging of the state personnel or the possibilities of transforming the organizational structure of the state apparatuses, as is often believed. They are in fact still more constrictive than this, for they sanction the 'continuity of the state' also by the institutional perpetuation of an effective *parallel state network*, which persists right through the various forms of bourgeois state, and which can also not be eliminated without 'smashing' the state apparatuses, i.e. without the transition to socialism (recall the Allende experiment in Chile). A *network*, as it runs through the various branches and apparatuses of the state; *parallel*, as it functions behind the facade of the state apparatuses, which carefully disguise it;

state, as although often only para-public, it provides a permanent recourse for the bourgeoisie in their struggle to
maintain and safeguard their power.

This network is therefore permanently present in the
bourgeois 'democracies' themselves (the example of the
United States or Germany could be given, to say nothing of
France or Italy), and it supplies the seeds of fascist development that are inherent to every form of the bourgeois state.
As against the hoary old notion of a radical opposition (in
kind) between 'totalitarianism' and 'democracy', the decisive
differences between exceptional regimes and bourgeois-
'democratic' ones should not lead us to forget that, beyond a
certain point, the limits to democratization are those of the
bourgeois state itself. This also shows that, contrary to a
theory of stages that would erect a Chinese wall between
'democratization' and 'socialism', a radical democratization
can only be attained by way of a genuine 'uninterrupted
process by stages towards socialism'.

It is now necessary to go into somewhat more detail on the
question of the internal contradictions within the dictatorships' apparatuses, having already established the effects these
have on the process of their overthrow. These contradictions
have so far been treated here principally as regards their
effects on the struggle of the popular masses, and particularly
that of the working class, but they must also be examined
from the point of view of their effects within the power bloc
itself, and also their effects on the relationship between the
power bloc and the petty bourgeoisie.

Such an analysis is all the more indispensable in so far as
the relationship between the possibility or otherwise of an
internal evolution of these regimes, and the role of their
internal contradictions in their overthrow, has not always been
well understood by the resistance organizations.

Two distinct and equally false positions have been put
forward. The first maintained that an internal evolution was
possible, attributing a disproportionate role to the dictatorships' internal contradictions. This was by and large the
typical position of Portuguese liberal and socialist circles

(including Mario Soares) at the beginning of the Caetano period, a position that Cunhal was correct to attack. The other position, more interesting for us here, maintained that an internal evolution of this kind was impossible, but at the same time minimized the role of internal contradictions. This indirectly emerges from Cunhal's own positions when he attacked, in 1965, the 'right-wing deviation' that the Portuguese Communist Party had experienced between 1956 and 1959:

'During the years 1956–59, the right-wing deviation expressed itself in the notion of a "peaceful solution to the political problem in Portugal", supposed to result from an allegedly irreversible and semi-automatic disintegration of the fascist regime. At that time, it was considered inevitable that the dictatorship would disappear in a short while as a result of its internal contradictions, and by the immediate, direct and mechanical influence of the changing balance of forces on the world scale . . . At various moments, putschist illusions, and particularly the hope that a military coup d'état by "dissidents within the regime" would put an end to the dictatorship, greatly influenced the practical activity of our party.'

It is clear from this passage that despite his correct positions on the impossibility of an internal evolution, Cunhal certainly under-estimated the role of internal contradictions.

What we can say more generally is that the impossibility of an internal evolution, and the need for a democratic break, in no way reduce the role of internal contradictions in setting in motion the process of this break.

We already established the consequences that the elimination of the bourgeoisie's own political organizations and parties had for this class. But even though parties are a privileged means of political organization for the bourgeoisie, they are not its only one. This makes for a decisive difference between the bourgeoisie and the working class. Bourgeois parties do not fulfil the same function for the bourgeoisie as revolutionary parties do for the working class. In the context of the bourgeois state, the latter are the workers' only means of organization. (This is precisely the meaning of the classical Marxist thesis of the need for an 'independent' organization of the working class.) For the power bloc, on the other hand, and the bourgeoisie in particular, even if political parties are still the privileged means of its organization, this role is supplemented by the entire spectrum of state apparatuses and branches, so that it is the capitalist state as such that appears as the power of the bourgeoisie organized as a dominant class. This theoretical interpretation was particularly developed by Gramsci, who saw the state as a whole as forming the 'party' of the dominant classes.

The political organization of the power bloc can therefore be supplied, in any form of the bourgeois state, by the state apparatuses as a whole, including both the ideological state apparatuses, whose principal role is the elaboration and inculcation of ideology, and the different branches of the repressive state apparatus (army, police, administration, judiciary, etc.), whose principal role is the exercize of repression. The result of this is that these various apparatuses and branches often come to form strongholds and privileged organizational bulwarks of this or that fraction of the bourgeoisie or component of the power bloc. Also relevant here is the fact that the capitalist state apparatuses often play an organizational role with respect to certain popular classes, which, without forming part of the power bloc, are often supporting classes for bourgeois power. This is the case with the petty bourgeoisie, and the popular classes in the country-side (the smallholding peasantry), which by not being basic classes of the capitalist social formation (these are simply the bourgeoisie and the working class), encounter considerable difficulties in organizing their own autonomous political parties. The state apparatuses that organize them often embody their support for the bourgeoisie by way of the 'power fetishism' characteristic of these classes.

It thus emerges that every bourgeois state is riven by contradictions between its various apparatuses and branches (and not just between political parties), as the organizational bases of one or other fraction and component of the power bloc. The contradictions most directly and acutely reflected within the state are those among the dominant classes and fractions, and the contradictions between these and the supporting classes, far more than the contradictions between the power bloc and the working class. The latter contradictions are basically expressed in the bourgeois state only 'at a distance', i.e. by a very mediated reproduction within the state. The contradictions among the fractions of the power bloc, on the other hand, are generally expressed by way of genuinely differentiated centres and bulwarks of power held by different fractions within the state. The unity of the state power, which in the last analysis is that of the hegemonic class or fraction within the power bloc, is expressed in a very complex fashion, by way of a contradictory domination of the branch or apparatus that particularly embodies this class or fraction's power and organization, over the other branches and apparatuses of the state.

This should enable us to grasp the internal contradictions within the military dictatorships, and cast light on what it is that distinguishes them from the parliamentary-democratic forms of state. In the case of these dictatorships, the contradictions between different apparatuses are expressed in a particular way, and with particular intensity.

We must remind ourselves here that these military dictatorships were not exclusively the representatives of the big comprador bourgeoisie, the oligarchy (big comprador bourgeoisie/landowners) or even, as far as the bourgeoisie is concerned, of monopoly capital alone. Under the hegemony of the big comprador bourgeoisie (in Greece) or the oligarchy in general (in Spain and Portugal), the bourgeoisie as a whole, including the domestic bourgeoisie and non-monopoly capital (not the same thing), continued to form part of the power bloc. This signifies that the internal contradictions were directly reflected within the state apparatuses, particularly within the dominant apparatus itself, i.e. the army.

We can add here too that, if the armed forces constitute the dominant apparatus in these regimes, which they do either directly, by proxy, or by the strict limits that they place on their functioning, this is because they control the fundamental levers of command and the centres of real power. This real power must be carefully distinguished from formal power, particularly in the case of these exceptional regimes, formal power being that which appears at the front of the political stage (the government), where the army officers are not always physically present. Neglecting to make this distinction, several writers have been led to under-estimate the real role of the armed forces, particularly in Portugal and Spain, where it was less conspicuously apparent (in Portugal above all) than was the case in Greece. It is certain, however, that the military apparatus, while always playing the dominant role, did not do so to the same extent in all three regimes, nor at all phases that they underwent, and this is expressed in the variable dominance of certain apparatuses over others. In Portugal, especially, the bureaucratic administration and the police apparatus (the PIDE), being relatively autonomous, progressively came to play a very important role, and this also happened, to a somewhat lesser degree, in Spain and in Greece. Furthermore, it would be a great mistake to believe that these regimes dismissed members of the dominant classes from their political personnel; various 'notables' and 'prominent personalities', who in every bourgeois state often participate directly in leading posts, did so here more than ever, by their presence in various coteries, pressure groups, clans and factions: an issue different from that of state power, which always remains the power of the dominant classes. The dominant role of the military, which is thus not only expressed in the visible institutional apparatus, also distinguishes these regimes from the fascist regimes proper, and this has a very particular result: the internal contradictions of these regimes are expressed above all in the military apparatus, the apparatus which above all others actually wields armed force (and not in the party and the bureaucracy, the dominant apparatuses of the fascist regimes). This all goes to make their internal contradictions still more formidable than is the case with the fascist regimes.

We come now to the way that these contradictions within

the power bloc are expressed in the military itself. In the absence of political parties, it is the military that becomes the privileged apparatus of political organization for the power bloc. In this process, the role of political parties for the bourgeoisie is replaced by that of the military, more precisely its upper echelons, which become the *de facto* political party of the bourgeoisie as a whole, under the direction of its hegemonic fraction. This process of substitution has its inherent limits. In the long run, the armed forces are unable to fulfil this role in any organic way; and this role is never more than relative, for other political representatives of the bourgeoisie still exist and continue to act, in a semi-clandestine way. But this substitution has a major consequence: the internal contradictions of the power bloc are directly reflected within the military, crystallizing in this or that tendency or faction, which supports this or that fraction of the power bloc. This is particularly clear in the case of the contradictions between the domestic bourgeoisie, on the one hand, and the big comprador bourgeoisie or oligarchy on the other, in the case of the Greek, Portuguese and Spanish armies, and even within their top echelons (the Greek military junta, and the military 'establishment' in Spain and Portugal). We need only refer to the contradictions between die-hard 'Atlanticists', 'Europeans', and supporters of an 'independent policy' oriented towards the Third World, which can now be seen as crystallizing the reproduction within the armed forces, by way of the internal factors (the power bloc), of the contradictions of capital on the international scale.

But the fact that the upper echelons of the armed forces tend to play the role of a political party for the bourgeoisie makes the contradictions of the power bloc particularly acute within the state. In actual fact, the operation of a 'pluralist' system of political parties in the parliamentary-democratic forms of the bourgeois state makes possible a ventilation and negotiated settlement of these contradictions. In the case of the dictatorships, not only do the upper echelons of the armed forces tend to become, as it were, the single party for the whole of the bourgeoisie, which in itself already involves an accentuation of internal contradictions, but this takes place precisely in the context of the particularly hierarchic, centralized and unitary ordering characteristic of the military. It follows that these contradictions crystallize and congeal into innumerable clans and factions, mutually eliminating one another under cover of maintaining the 'unity' of the armed forces. Moreover, because of this hierarchic, disciplined and centralized organization, and the particular form of ideological circulation that it involves, it happens that whole sections of the armed forces from top to bottom, including the lower echelons, follow the various leading clans which crystallize the contradictions within the power bloc. These are then expressed in the form of oppositions between vertical segments of the military apparatus: oppositions between the three services, such as were particularly clear-cut in Greece at the time of the abortive naval putsch of May 1973, and also in Portugal; between the *guardia civil* and the army in Spain, expressed in open conflict in the hours and days following the death of Carrero Blanco; and between the various divisions and corps that make up the army in Greece.

We must now return to the particular role that the military can play with respect to other social classes, in particular the petty bourgeoisie. Even when this class is not, at least as a whole, a supporting class for the regime (which was never the case in Greece, and gradually ceased to be so in Spain and Portugal), i.e. even when the army is not the direct political organizer of this class, it still maintains close ties with the petty bourgeoisie, and this is particularly the case for a section of its middle and lower ranks. These ties are originally based on class origin (Greece, Spain, and Portugal after the reform of the military academy in 1958) and class membership (in the Spanish case, in particular, the low level of pay means that the great majority of officers even have a parallel civilian job), but their significance goes far beyond this basis. In every case, given the constitutional inability of the petty bourgeoisie to give itself its own independent political apparatuses, these ties form genuine politico-ideological ties of representation. Thus the contradictions between petty bourgeoisie and bourgeoisie cut through the armed forces in a far more direct way than do those between the bourgeoisie and the working class, and they are intensified by the fact that the upper echelons of the armed forces become the direct political representatives of the bourgeoisie, substituting themselves in a complex way for the banned or eliminated political parties. Added to the class determination of these upper echelons (embourgeoisement), this still further reinforces the cleavages between them and the lower levels.

These internal contradictions between bourgeoisie and petty bourgeoisie are articulated to those of the power bloc, and intensify them. The evolution of a large section of the petty bourgeoisie towards open opposition to the military regimes directly affected certain strata of the armed forces, whether in the direction of mere disaffection with the regime, or in that of declared opposition in one form or another. In Greece, we had the captains' movement in the Northern army, but also the support given by certain middle and lower echelons of the air force, and even the navy, to the pronunciamento of a group of generals and admirals against the junta; in Portugal, the Armed Forces Movement, very different in form.

The Portuguese Armed Forces Movement, while very divided internally, is still on the whole more of a movement corresponding to a clear-cut radicalization of the petty bourgeoisie towards the left, than a movement representing the class positions of the working class. Several indices show this: the recent economic programme of the AFM, which is far from envisaging structural transformations involving a 'break', even of the anti-monopoly type; the economic policy actually carried out so far under its aegis; and above all the undoubtable mistrust that a section of the AFM shows towards any popular movements other than those in direct support of its own initiatives, a mistrust that is far from just affecting reputed 'ultra-leftists'. Although the AFM's programme speaks of serving the 'interests of the working classes', this is not exactly expressed in the decree of 27th August 1974, published after the dismissal of Palma

Carlos, and under the premiership of Vasco Gonçalves, member of the AFM's Coordinating Committee. Though it has not yet been applied (or could not be applied), this decree, which is still in force, places draconian limitations on the right to strike. In particular, it lays down a statutory period of thirty-seven days that must elapse between the beginning of an industrial conflict and the actual commencement of a strike; it specifies that strikes that do not respect statutory arrangements or seek to alter a contract already in force are unlawful, as well as strikes called for political or religious reasons (an old story), solidarity strikes with another industry or trade, and finally 'isolated stoppages of labour in strategic sectors of a firm whose aim is the disorganization of production'. While allowing picketing, the decree forbids strikers to occupy places of work and recognizes the right of management in firms where illegal strikes take place to call a lock-out. There can be no doubt that this represents a compromise with the domestic bourgeoisie, and that the spectre of the Chilean '*gremios*' is evoked for a reason. It still remains that this decree, alongside which even the Karamanlis constitution seems like extravagant liberalism, would not be possible without the complex relationship between an important section of the AFM and the positions of the petty bourgeoisie. Other indications can also be noted, e.g. the often ambiguous and suspicious attitude of COPCON towards working-class demands and movements of *saneamento* from below; the fact that, while the AFM, in a somewhat surprising evolution, has opened its ranks to career NCOs, it still remains closed to conscript officers and to rank-and-file soldiers, etc.

To sum up, in the opportunities that the armed forces originally created for the overthrow of the Greek and Portuguese dictatorships, we find a conjunction between sectors representing the positions of the domestic bourgeoisie, and those representing the petty bourgeoisie. This is an alliance between two sectors within the armed forces themselves, both in Greece and in Portugal. In the latter country this alliance is still holding, for better or worse, and despite its characteristic instability. It exists both between the section of the military hierarchy that follows President Costa Gomes (the 'professionalist' tendency, several officers close to the Socialist Party and the PPD, etc.), and also within the AFM itself, between the Higher Council, which even includes old sympathizers of Spinola from the Junta of National Salvation (men such as Almeida Bruno and Mario Monge who were active supporters of Spinola in the past, are still prominent members of the AFM), and the Coordinating Commission (Gonçalves, Carvalho, etc.), which is far more radicalized. The Commission represents, within the AFM's general assembly, the positions of those 40 per cent or so of delegates favouring an anti-capitalist policy. A fact to be noted is that the present expansion of the AFM in no way means a general radicalization of the Portuguese armed forces. An accompaniment of it is that this conflictual alliance within the military is more and more manifest within the AFM itself, to the extent that this tends to become the dominant structure in the armed forces. The alliance between domestic bourgeoisie and petty bourgeoisie in the Portuguese forces broadly crystallizes, at the present moment (for there is undoubtedly a radicalization of a section of the AFM, concomitant with its opening to lower ranks), the polarization, in the process of overthrowing the dictatorship, of a significant section of the petty bourgeoisie towards the domestic bourgeoisie.

We can draw two lessons from the above analysis;

a) The popular masses can find genuine support and even allies within the armed forces in their struggle against the dictatorships (and this is also the case with regard to other state apparatuses). This naturally means a policy on their part which does not simply amalgamate the armed forces as a whole (and the agents of all other state apparatuses) with the 'enemy'. As far as the Greek and Spanish forces are concerned, despite their former participation in bloody civil wars against the popular masses, the slogan that gradually came to prevail in the left-wing organizations was that of 'national reconciliation' on the basis of national independence, and this made a big contribution towards sharpening the splits in their ranks.

b) Both on account of the specific organizational features of the armed forces, and their politico-ideological ties of representation with various different classes, the splits within them occur in a very complex manner. We must guard here against simplistic notions, as if the top echelons formed a unified bloc behind one or other fraction of the power bloc (comprador bourgeoisie, oligarchy), and the middle and lower ranks were similarly united behind the petty bourgeoisie. For the armed forces are also divided vertically right the way down. The popular masses may find support at the top (domestic bourgeoisie) as well as at the lower levels, while their enemies may be located in these lower levels as well as at the top (comprador bourgeoisie, oligarchy). Although it is certainly in the middle and lower ranks that the hard core of popular support will most often be found, it should not be forgotten that the spearhead of the regime's praetorian guard may be found in the same milieu, such as the military police batallions of General Ioannidis in Greece, conscripts recruited for the most part from worker and peasant families. This is due both to the specific discipline of the military apparatus, and to the refraction (specific reproduction) of petty-bourgeois positions within its ranks. Given the class nature of the petty bourgeoisie, its internal divisions and its 'vacillations', while one section of it is radicalized to the left, a further section is radicalized and 'swings' towards the right. This is reflected within the military, where the latter section can provide a base for the 'ultras' and their shock-troops. A further factor, particularly in the Portuguese case, is the reflection within the armed forces of the divisions between the popular classes in the countryside. One section of these, polarized towards the big landed proprietors by way of the surviving vestiges of feudal ideological and socio-political relations, and under pressure from certain sectors of the Church, continues to support the old regime. Certain sections of conscripts in Portugal, and NCOs in particular, still bear strong resemblance to the French 'Versaillais' troops of 1871.

The internal contradictions of the armed forces thus reflect and reproduce class contradictions, but they cannot be reduced to the latter, any more than can those in other apparatuses. The reproduction of class contradictions within the armed forces, and the state apparatuses in general, takes place in a specific and mediated way, combining with the specific characteristics of each of these apparatuses and its functions. This is the context in which certain other factors are located, which also contribute towards this complexity in the reproduction of class contradictions within the apparatuses, and within the armed forces in particular.

1. First of all, the various cliques, factions and clans, a special form in which class contradictions are refracted under these regimes, come to acquire a relative autonomy of their own in relation to the classes in struggle. The exceptional state displays the features of relative autonomy that are specific to the capitalist state in general in the context of the instability and disequilibrium of class relations corresponding to its own particular form. The relative autonomy vis-à-vis this or that fraction of the power bloc, which is necessary for the capitalist state in order to secure the unstable equilibrium of compromise on which are based both the hegemony of one class or fraction over others within the power bloc, and that of this bloc as a whole over the popular masses, assumes a special form in this case. As I have dealt with this phenomenon elsewhere (for the particular case of fascism), I shall speak here only of its effects on the regimes we are concerned with at the moment. It gives rise here to a specific margin of autonomy for the various different apparatuses which embody it, in particular the armed forces, and makes possible a struggle between various clans, factions and coteries which does not entirely coincide, in a direct and mechanical way, with the class contradictions. Given the important role that falls to the military in the real levers of state command ('real' power), this struggle hinges on corporative interests and privileges of various kinds: the distribution of state funds, material benefits of various kinds, division of influence and power within the state, etc. Frictions of this kind are certainly

similar to those existing in every capitalist state, but the particular relative autonomy of the exceptional state endows them with a specific degree of intensity.

If it is wrong to believe, as certain writers do, that the army rules, in the military dictatorships, to promote 'its own' interests, subordinating even the dominant classes themselves, it is still the case that the reproduction of class contradictions within the armed forces is articulated in these various clans and factions onto a secondary friction and struggle due to corporate interests of this kind. This both contributes to the complexity of the reproduction of class contradictions, and is also a factor in intensifying the internal contradictions in the armed forces. Two particularly telling examples of this can be given here. In Greece, a whole series of major contradictions in the armed forces led to massive purges and retirements under the military dictatorship, which were due among other things to the swelling of the upper ranks and the promotion difficulties of the generation of officers (colonels) commissioned at an accelerated pace during the Civil War (1946–49). In Portugal, the armed forces movement against the dictatorship was catalyzed by a blunder on the part of the Caetano government concerning the corporate interests of career officers: the decree of July 1973, designed to promote the incorporation into the forces of a larger number of conscripts, introduced a differential calculation of seniority for conscript and career officers. These latter, mobilized on the corporate basis of defending their privileges, were rapidly involved in the political challenge being planned by a small core of officers.

2. The complex way in which class contradictions under the military dictatorships are refracted within the armed forces also bears on another factor. To the same extent that there is a process of relative substitution, the armed forces taking the place of political parties, the ideological role of the military assumes a growing importance. It is true that the military has an ideological role in every bourgeois state, parallel with its repressive role, but in the parliamentary-democratic forms

this role remains in general a secondary one in the forming of the dominant ideology. In the regimes we are dealing with here, however, where the 'bourgeois' political parties are eliminated as ideological state apparatuses, and the armed forces become the dominant apparatus in the state, thus taking on the parallel mission of legitimating the regime, this ideological role increases considerably, a process concomitant with the growth of their repressive role.

This has two consequences: a) contradictions within the power bloc, and between the power bloc and the popular classes, are reproduced within the armed forces by way of ideological variations within the apparatus; b) this mediation of class contradictions is embodied by way of the military apparatus's own specific internal ideology, the specific form that the dominant ideology assumes within this apparatus.

Let us dwell firstly on the army's nationalism. Nationalist ideology is of considerable importance in the military apparatus, because of its specific role in the very constitution of the bourgeois national state, in the process of the bourgeois-democratic revolution and in the organization of 'national unity'. The ambiguities and metamorphoses of nationalism are very familiar: in the imperialist stage, this has gradually come to take a highly reactionary aspect in the dominant countries, while in the dominated countries, by way of their demands for 'national liberation', it has assumed a progressive aspect. What we are concerned with here is particularly the nationalism of the present phase of imperialism, as this affects the European countries in general, and those we are dealing with here in particular. To put it rather summarily, the new dependence of the European countries vis-à-vis the dominant imperialism of the United States means that nationalism can now again have a certain progressive character in these countries, even though they do not belong to the traditional zone of the Third World or the 'under-developed' countries, but actually form part of the dominant sphere; this was the case with certain progressive aspects of Gaullist nationalism in France. It is all the more true for the countries we are concerned with here. While they no longer belong to the so-called 'under-developed' zone and even function as a staging-post (Greece, Portugal) for the exploitation of the African continent by the dominant countries, they are still marked by a characteristic dependence vis-à-vis the centres of imperialism.

It is useful therefore to examine the evolution of nationalist ideology in the Greek, Spanish and Portuguese armed forces. During an initial period (from the nineteenth to the early twentieth century in Spain and Portugal, and from the beginning of the twentieth century up to around 1935 in Greece), these often played a positive role, intervening openly in processes of the bourgeois-democratic revolution type by way of a progressive nationalism. In a second period, encompassing the civil wars in Spain and Greece, the Cold War, the role of NATO, etc., these forces underwent a massive turn, in one form or another, towards imperialist and ultra-reactionary nationalism. In the present phase, corresponding to the new dependence of these countries, certain sectors of the armed forces, particularly in Greece and Portugal, have gradually seen the rebirth, if in a highly confused manner, of the progressive aspect of nationalism in a new form, one marked by demands for independence and national sovereignty in the face of other sectors and leading circles who have remained in thrall to a viciously reactionary Atlanticism (the Greek, Spanish and Portuguese nations as 'motherlands' of the 'Christian West'). The confused renascence of this new nationalism has long been under-estimated by the left and its organizations. We can take the example of the Greek withdrawal from the NATO military organization, which evoked a favourable response from the Greek army. While the American attitude in the Cyprus affair was largely responsible for this, it should not be forgotten that the colonels' regime saw constant friction between 'Atlanticists' and 'independents' (or even 'third-worldists') in the armed forces.

An interesting point here is that these demands for national sovereignty and independence have been skilfully exploited by the domestic bourgeoisie, as they serve its interests in its contradictions with the comprador bourgeoisie – 'exploited', for the interests of the domestic bourgeoisie are far from corresponding to effective national autonomy in regard to all foreign dependence (including that on the Common Market). On the other hand, however, these demands by certain sectors of the Greek and Portuguese armed forces have coincided to a certain extent with the genuine demand for 'national liberation' raised by the radicalized petty bourgeoisie, the proletarianized rural masses and the working class. In other words, this aspect of nationalism is the principal way in which the class positions of the domestic bourgeoisie and the popular classes are refracted within the armed forces, and it is through nationalism of this kind that the humiliation of the Portuguese army in its colonial wars, and that of the Greek army in the Cyprus affair, were experienced. This explains among other things why this national humiliation did not provoke a revolt similar to that of the French OAS after the Algerian war, in the name of 'Western civilization'.

But the very nature of nationalism means that this process has involved serious difficulties and ambiguities. The armies involved were previously gripped by the spirit of the Cold War and NATO, and added to this in Spain and Greece are the sequels of the civil war, this very nationalism being combined with a deep 'anti-communism' (in the broad sense in which the communists are 'anti-national'). The 'progressive' nationalist sections in the armed forces are often themselves moved simultaneously, in one and the same current, by the concern for national independence and by anti-communism, and this is still perceptible, underneath surface appearances, in the 'progressive' sectors of the Portuguese army itself. Moreover, in certain sectors of the army, demands for national independence are often allied with an aggressive expansionist nationalism, giving rise to extremely ambiguous ideological phenomena. I need only mention here what has quite incorrectly been described as the 'Kadhafi-ist' tendency in the Greek army, strongly in favour of '*enosis*', and the intervention in Cyprus against Makarios; this is far from the most Atlanticist tendency in the Greek army, even though it is notorious that the putsch against Makarios was ultimately planned by the CIA.

One final feature has also played a paradoxical role for these regimes: the army as the pillar of 'order' – not just in the repressive sense, but also in that of the 'continuity of the state' and 'national unity'. This paradox lies in the fact that from originally cementing the army behind the establishment and preservation of the dictatorship, this ideology contributed in the long run to the disaffection of certain sectors of the armed forces. These regimes showed themselves so incapable of transformation at a time when political contradictions and crises were intensifying, that their very existence eventually came to appear to whole sections of the armed forces as a danger to the continuity of the state and to national unity, creating the conditions for a general explosion. This factor had a great significance, even for certain upper echelons, who thereby became disaffected with the regime. It also marks, however, the limits and ambiguities involved in the over-throw of the dictatorships. Firstly, it is evident that these sections only sided against the regime on condition that the 'continuity of the state' was preserved, and even in order to preserve this, and this is one reason for the limits imposed on democratic transformations and purges. Secondly, and this is just as evident, certain of these sections placed their bets on political organizations of the popular masses, at least for the transition period, and on the Communist Parties in particular, as factors of 'order' which would help confine popular strug-gles within 'reasonable' bounds, linking up in this way with the designs of the domestic bourgeoisies. The Portuguese case is particularly instructive in this respect, and involved far more than Spinola and his entourage. This can only be an explosively ambiguous situation.

The internal contradictions of these regimes, however, do not just affect the armed forces, but also, if to different degrees, the great majority of ideological apparatuses, as well as other branches of the repressive apparatus. The same principles that governed the above analysis of internal contradictions within the armed forces can in fact also be applied, *mutatis mutandis*, to the analysis of these other apparatuses. Here, too,

we have the contradictions within the power bloc, and between this and the popular masses, particularly the working
class and petty bourgeoisie; the ties of political representation
that are formed, in the absence of political parties, both
between the upper echelons of these apparatuses and the
power bloc (the cases of the judiciary, administration, Church,
press and publishing, education, corporatist trade unions,
etc.), and between the popular masses, the petty bourgeoisie
in particular, and the middle and lower levels; and the complex refraction of these contradictions by way of the specific
characteristics, internal ideology and particular corporate
interests of the agents of each of these apparatuses. I shall
just give a few examples of this.

1. There is first of all the case of the contradictions of the
religious apparatus, the Catholic Church, which are particularly significant in the Portuguese and Spanish cases. In
Spain, these even led to a complete transformation in the
attitude of a major section of this apparatus towards the
Franco regime. This transformation was certainly due in
part to the new policy of the Vatican in the last few years (the
so-called '*aggiornamento*'), but what is far more important
for us here are its internal causes in both Spain and Portugal.
Just as in several other European countries, the Church used
to form the chief organizational bastion within the state for
the big landed proprietors, in the process of capitalist development and as an ideological state apparatus in this. To this
extent, it was directly involved in the establishment and
perpetuation of the dictatorships in Spain and Portugal (the
so-called oligarchy of big landed property and the comprador
bourgeoisie).

In the relationships between its 'hierarchy', i.e. its top
echelons, and the power bloc, the decline in both the economic
position of the landlords and their political weight within the
power bloc was the first reason for the Church's relative
disaffection, particularly in Spain, where the decline of the
landlords was far more clear than in Portugal (a process
somewhat analogous to that experienced by the Catholic

Church under Italian fascism). Added to this were the repercussions within the Church hierarchy of the new compromise attempted between the comprador bourgeoisie and the domestic bourgeoisie (Opus Dei). As far as the middle and lower levels are concerned, the upsurge of popular mass struggle, not only by the working class and the petty bourgeoisie in the towns, but also involving the gradual disaffection of broad sections of the poor and middle peasantry due to the proletarianization of the countryside, affected them directly. This was expressed in the forms specific to the ideology of this apparatus, by the replacement of 'Christ the King' by the 'poor and proletarian' Christ, but in a complex manner and with certain lower-level members of this apparatus (the Portuguese rural clergy in particular) continuing to count among the most traditionalist elements. Nevertheless, in a situation where one section of the religious apparatus kept up its support for the oligarchy, this process led in Spain to internal splits of such severity that it may well be asked whether there are not now really two churches in Spain. This is all the more important a development for the dictatorships in so far as the religious apparatus is one of the most basic of the ideological state apparatuses.

In Greece the process was rather different. For a long while, the religious apparatus (the Orthodox Church) has only played a secondary ideological role, partly because of the rapid elimination of big landed property at the beginning of the century, this having always been relatively limited in the Greek case. The persistent attempts by the colonels to get the Church to play a more significant ideological role were totally without success. In the absence of any centre such as the Vatican, the junta was relatively successful in its brutal intervention to replace a large section of bishops, particularly the Archbishop of Athens, by its own stooges, but the lower clergy, who have always been very close to the people and their struggles (as was very clear during the resistance to the Nazi invasion), remained by and large obstinately opposed to the dictatorship. This explains why the junta's interventions in the religious apparatus gave rise to explosive contradictions. They actually gave rise to a really indescribable disorder, which played a modest part in the disintegration of the regime.

2. Analogous internal contradictions also appeared in the state's 'bureaucratic' administration under these regimes, and this was an apparatus that had come to play a very important role. Without repeating here the points already made, I will just indicate the new elements in these contradictions.

First of all, the contradictions within the power bloc are expressed in the top ranks of the administrative apparatus in a particularly confused way, on account of the new dominant ideology within this apparatus in the present phase of imperialism. The dominant ideology now shifts from the juridico-political domain (embodiment of the general will, civil liberties, etc.) towards the economic domain, particularly in the form of technocracy (the 'technocrats' of the Spanish and Greek regimes in particular, but also those under Caetano). By its apparently apolitical character, this ideology of technocracy enabled the top ranks of the state administration to give direct and massive support to regimes that actively contributed towards the new dependence of these countries on imperialism, corresponding with their accelerated industrialization. These elements saw in the dictatorship special factors of 'technical progress' and 'modernization' ('developmentalism'). It was only when the inherent contradictions of this process came more and more clearly to the fore that a section of these top ranks took their distance from the dictatorship, most frequently still within the problematic of technocracy, considering it initially as simply 'inefficient'. Their gradual awareness of the regime's dependence on imperialist capital was largely the result of the development of contradictions between the domestic and the comprador bourgeoisie.

As far as the contradictions between the top echelons of the administration and the intermediate and lower levels are concerned, a further and seemingly paradoxical factor can be added: the attempts made by these regimes themselves to 'rationalize' the operation of the bureaucracy. This process was in fact a contradictory one. Based as they are on a strict disciplinary control of the administration by a 'bureaucratic', centralized and archaic mode of operation, these regimes are incapable of proceeding with any major reform of it, such as is required by the 'development of under-development' in the new phase of imperialist dependence. This all helps to intensify the contradictions of the process of dependent industrialization, and also provokes the hostility of the domestic bourgeoisie. Limited attempts in this direction were made none the less, in Greece and Spain in particular, arising from these regimes' relationship with the domestic bourgeoisie. These attempts, involving for example the attenuation of bureaucratic hierarchies, the renewal of administrative elites, etc., certainly went together with a reinforcement of political control over the administration by the assignment to key posts of officials completely loyal to the regime, but they still attested to the genuine need for 'rationalization', i.e. for the adaptation of the state administration to the new phase of imperialism (establishment of a 'technocratic-authoritarian' complex). This process, however, directly challenged the entire series of corporate privileges enjoyed by the traditional officialdom, an old and parasitic refuge for the children of proletarianized peasants and petty bourgeois in the face of endemic unemployment, and it thereby intensified their contradictions with the regime. A similar process, indicating the impossibility of modernizing the state, is also at work in other European countries, even if it takes rather different forms and proportions.

We should finally mention the effect that the veritable pillage of state funds by the bourgeoisie and the leading circles of these 'pure and hard' regimes has on administration agents who are still strongly imbued with the ideology of the 'general interest' and 'public welfare'. Although the secrecy and censorship that surround the state's functioning favour practices of this kind and prevent them from becoming fully known, the long-run effect, when they are divulged, ends up by provoking real ruptures within the administration, all the more so in that these regimes constantly present themselves as the absolute embodiment of 'incorruptibility', as opposed to the 'rottenness' and 'peculation' of the 'politicians' (viz. the Matesa affair in Spain, and the scandals involving the import of diseased meat in Greece).

3. The educational apparatus, and the universities in particular, is also afflicted with very substantial contradictions between its upper echelons and the intermediate and lower levels of the teaching staff. These are fundamentally due to the prodigious upsurge of student and intellectual struggles, which in exceptional cases have even affected certain agents at the very top of this apparatus. There are analogies here with what has happened in other European countries, but under the dictatorships these contradictions are intensified as a result of such factors as the almost feudal structure of the universities, though this in itself goes back far beyond the era of these regimes. It goes together with the weakness of the bourgeoisie and its lack of organic intellectuals (as in Greece), or the close integration of the bourgeoisie with a landed oligarchy (as in Spain and Portugal), where the Church has a correspondingly strong influence. In these cases, the 'liberal' bourgeois reforms that took place prior to the dictatorships did not even touch the university apparatus. By way of successive purges, these regimes simply reinforced the terrorist dictatorship, both corporative and intellectual, of the professors (the notorious *catedraticos* in Spain) over the teaching staff as a whole. Added to this are the effects that the rise of the domestic bourgeoisie had even within the top ranks of the university apparatuses, certain of the personnel affected being converted to a technocratic-style 'liberalism', and in Spain in particular, the changes in the attitude of the Church, so that a number of higher education establishments under its control, particularly those of the Jesuits, came to be more liberal than those of the state sector.

4. Finally, considerable internal contradictions also appeared, for analogous reasons, within a whole series of other

apparatuses. This was the case with the civilian judges and lawyers in Greece, and more recently in Spain, in their opposition to the permanent role of military justice and tribunals, and also to the characteristic 'arbitrariness' of the legal system under these regimes, which eventually ended up by affronting even the professional lawyers' legalistic conception of justice. A particular case in point is the vanguard role that the lawyers' associations gradually came to play in the struggle for freedom.

In the press, the constant about-turns of these regimes on the question of a liberalization of censorship led to the appearance of contradictions related to the struggles of intellectuals (writers, journalists, etc.), and especially to the fact that the domestic bourgeoisie often turned towards this apparatus in its search for autonomous bases of political organization (which was clearly the case in both Spain and Greece). The role of the press and publishing here was analogous to that which this played for the bourgeoisie in its struggle against the landed aristocracy and the absolutist regimes in the period preceding the bourgeois-democratic revolutions in Europe.

Within the corporatist trade-union apparatus, constantly in crisis and the throes of reorganization, these contradictions related to the struggles of the working class, the implantation of left-wing militants and the strategies of various fractions of the power bloc vis-à-vis working-class militancy.

Within the state economic apparatus, they were directly related to the contradictions between the domestic bourgeoisie and the comprador bourgeoisie. For example, certain aspects favourable to this bourgeoisie of the INI's policy in Spain; in Portugal, the policy of R. Martins which led to the draft legislation of the *Fomento Industrial*, though this remained for the most part unapplied; in Greece, the policy of certain technocrats in the planning apparatus. These contradictions crystallized in political differences over the question of foreign investment, among other things.

It should be borne in mind that these contradictions within the state apparatuses of the military dictatorships only had the described effects in setting under way the processes that overthrew these regimes, by virtue of their accumulation and condensation. The characteristic arbitrariness of the dictatorships gives them forceful means of eliminating such contradictions when these arise in isolation, if only by police control in the recruitment of the state agents, and by successive and constant purges. But besides the fact that these terrorist measures in the long run only accelerate the contradictions in question, there is nothing they can do in a conjuncture in which the regime is in crisis and the contradictions accumulate and condense together. Devoid of any mass base, the dictatorship cannot meet the upsurge of mass struggle with a concentrated purge, for fear of causing a total disorganization of the state which would put in question the capitalist system itself.

In bringing this analysis of the military dictatorships' internal contradictions to a close, there is one final point I should like to make, bearing once again on the difference between these regimes and the fascist regimes proper. In our case, it is not only within each apparatus that contradictions arise, but also in the relationships between each apparatus and the rest. This also happens under the fascist regimes, but with a major distinction that bears on the particular role of fascist ideology; this plays a definite role in cementing the cohesion of the various apparatuses, which are deeply imbued with it. On the basis of this ideology, the fascist regimes establish one particular apparatus (the fascist party) which, besides its role vis-à-vis the popular masses, also functions, in parallel always with police control, as an apparatus which in some degree 'caps' the others and maintains their cohesion.

There is nothing comparable with this in the regimes we are concerned with here. These lack both the specific cohesion of the parliamentary-democratic regimes' apparatuses, a cohesion which functions not by cementing a monolithic bloc, but because it corresponds to an organic circulation of class hegemony within the apparatuses, and they also lack the unifying apparatus of the whole institutional establishment that the fascist party provides.

In the long run, therefore, and given the institutional centralization of power, class contradictions, contradictions between the various corporate interests of the members of each apparatus, and those between the ideological sub-systems specific to each of these, also crystallize in very significant contradictions between the various apparatuses: between the military and other apparatuses (administration, university, press, judiciary), between the administration and other apparatuses (university, press, judiciary), between the Church and other apparatuses, and so on. Added to these contradictions and intensifying them, are the internal con-tradictions of each apparatus, and this renders the military dictatorships more vulnerable than the fascist regimes, chiefly on account of the opportunities provided for the popular masses to exploit these contradictions. This character-istic absence of politico-ideological cohesion between the various apparatuses of the military dictatorships aided the spectacular infiltration of the Portuguese corporatist unions by Communist militants, and we may also note the ever growing presence of left-wing militants in the Spanish universities.

The military dictatorships seek to remedy this state of affairs in a number of ways, and this is an additional reason for the existence of the various clans and coteries, which generally realign the leading agents of the various apparatuses and thus tend to form themselves into inter-apparatus centres of cohesion. Other forms also appear alongside this. In Greece, for example, we had the presence of either active officers, or more often retired generals, at different command posts throughout the apparatuses. All these means are however of limited effectiveness in relation to the role that a genuine fascist party can play. On the one hand, because of the open struggle that the various coteries and factions wage among themselves, without this being slotted into a specific organiza-tional framework; on the other hand, because of the resistance that the agents of one apparatus (the military) encounter, in the absence of a unifying ideology, at their command posts in other apparatuses which still have their own ideological sub-systems – even at the top levels. The nomination of actual military governors at the head of the Greek universities, for instance, deeply angered a number of their leading agents, even though these were themselves untarnished conservatives, if not downright reactionaries.

In the context of a crisis of regime, then, the delicate arbitration of internal conflicts by an ultimate summit that the centralization of power implies simply can not operate in the absence of an organization such as the fascist party. Far from being based on the 'charismatic power' of a 'providential leader', this arbitration always has to be embodied by transmission belts and institutional relays, and in this situation, these rapidly disintegrate.

VI

Conclusion

I have tried in this essay to indicate the paths taken by the process of democratization, though this analysis in no way seeks to prejudge the future of these social formations. Given in particular the force of the popular movement unleashed by the overthrow of the dictatorships, and developing in the course of the democratization process, the question of a transition to socialism is still as acute as ever, in the specific conditions of dependence experienced by these countries. It is by no means certain, in other words, whether the stage of democratization can be consolidated as such in the long run, in this highly unstable situation, and whether the bourgeoisie will succeed, as it has done in other European countries, in blocking the rise of revolutionary conjunctures for a long period. This is particularly the case in Portugal.

This immediately raises a further question. Are there grounds for fearing a relapse or return to exceptional regimes in one form or other, not necessarily the same as before? It emerges quite clearly from everything that has so far been said that this danger is far from over. The regimes overthrown have handed down a substantial legacy, and the limits of democratization still enable powerful forces of reaction to exist as a 'reserve' for the bourgeoisie. These forces will probably continue to exist for a long while, and they are certainly not a reserve force for the 'Republic'.

It goes without saying that these reactionary forces will remain vigilant, and ready to intervene when the question of a transition to socialism is historically posed (and not just in words). This is the least doubtful, as far as they are concerned. But it can also not be ruled out that these forces will intervene with a view to halting the democratization process, before the question of a socialist transition is even raised (viz. Spinola's attempt in September 1974, or the abortive military putsch in Greece in February 1975). In point of fact, exceptional regimes do not just come into being as a 'hot' reaction to a development towards socialism and national independence that is already under way or even imminent. It is true that, in the countries we are concerned with, neither the hegemony of the bourgeoisie, nor its compromises with the comprador bourgeoisie and with foreign capital, have as yet been radically threatened by the democratization process, and this, taken together with the power and organization of the popular movement developing in this process, seriously restrains the possibilities of a Pinochet-style reaction. But even the democratization process already signifies a redistribution of power relations and a certain limitation of both the prerogatives wielded up to now by the comprador bourgeoisie and foreign capital, and of the overwhelming role of the United States.

Experience shows that this limitation, or even the renegotiation of the equilibrium of compromise, may sometimes be enough to provoke a putschist reaction from the comprador bourgeoisie, foreign imperialist capital and the United States, these forces not being so readily disposed to let such matters pass. As far as the domestic bourgeoisie is concerned, given its internal divisions, economic dependence and politico-ideological weakness, it is generally incapable of putting up a unified resistance to such a reaction from the comprador bourgeoisie and foreign capital. In situations of such acute crisis, large fractions of the domestic bourgeoisie soon come to place themselves under the protection of the reactionary forces. In actual fact, the domestic bourgeoisie is itself afraid of events getting out of hand, or even of a rise in class struggle; it can also be tempted by a regime of 'preventive war' against the popular masses. And this is not all. In certain cases, the hesitations and divisions of the domestic bourgeoisie may rapidly be reflected among broad sections of the petty bourgeoisie, which is still to an appreciable extent polarized towards this bourgeoisie. The petty bourgeoisie may also be directly involved in the bourgeoisie's measures of economic sabotage, as was the case in Chile.

A second point here bears on the very nature of those regimes that have replaced the dictatorships in the democratic stage, or are on the point of doing so in the case of Spain. I have spoken here of the replacement of the dictatorships by 'parliamentary-democratic' regimes. But in employing this classic and customary term, I have only used it in an indicative way, so as to demarcate the difference, within the bourgeois state itself, between the exceptional state (one of *open war* against the popular masses) and the bourgeois-'democratic' forms. The expression 'parliamentary-democratic', as applied to the regimes that have replaced these dictatorships, should not be understood as referring to a traditional form of regime in which parliament really is dominant. There are two reasons for this.

a) A general reason, which to a greater or lesser extent affects all the capitalist countries in the present phase of imperialism. These countries have experienced a whole series of structural transformations (economic, political and ideological), which the present capitalist crisis is simply accelerating, and these have considerable effects on every capitalist state. In particular, the institutionalization of a whole 'technocratic-authoritarian' complex, concomitant among other things with the endemic crisis of the bourgeois classes as a whole in the face of the global upsurge of popular struggles. This does not just involve a further strengthening of the executive in relation to parliament, but actually heralds the end of a certain form of 'political democracy' as such, as a result of the transformations that this process involves. It is evident enough that the 'democratic' character of these regimes (as distinct from the exceptional regimes) cannot be measured against some ideal of the parliamentary regime which now belongs in the past. The regimes that have replaced the dictatorships already present in the Greek case, and will sooner or later do so in Portugal, unless events there take a quite different turn, certain of the technocratic-authoritarian features characteristic of the present phase of imperialism. These features should not lead one to under-estimate their difference from the exceptional regimes which they have replaced, no more than the transformations which the other capitalist countries are now undergoing can be identified with a 'rise of fascism' there. The relationship and the difference between the exceptional form of state and the other forms of the bourgeois state must always be seen in relation to the phase in which these forms appear and develop. Thus while the German and Italian fascist regimes were clearly distinct from the 'democratic' regimes of the other capitalist countries, the latter still themselves proceeded, in the 1930s, with a considerable structural reinforcement of the executive vis-à-vis both parliament and civil liberties.

b) Furthermore, the difference between the exceptional form of the bourgeois state and its other forms cannot be viewed simply in relation to the present phase of imperialism as a whole, but must also be seen in relation to the position that the countries involved occupy in the imperialist chain; it is this place that determines certain particular features of the class struggle in the different countries involved. In the case of the dominated and dependent countries, this differ-ence must be understood in relation to the zone of dependence; it cannot be compared mechanically with the situation in the dominant countries. In a superficial and Europocentric comparison with 'Western democracy', it is clear that the regimes of the dominated and dependent countries are all more or less far removed from this ideal-typical model, and in such a comparison they might all seem to be exceptional regimes. This can lead on the one hand to an under-estimation of the decisive difference between the exceptional form of state (that of open war) and the other forms of the bourgeois state, in the sense that these terms have for the dominated countries. To take a simple example, there is a considerable difference between Mexico, which is still far from a 'Western democracy', and Pinochet's Chile. On the other hand, it can give the impression that the present phase of imperialism inevitably condemns the dominated countries to fascism, bonapartism or military dictatorship, as the only alternative to a simple transition to socialism.

By virtue of the particular character of the class struggle in the dominated countries, this phase really does give rise to a new type of dependent capitalist state, even though the various forms and regimes of this display certain basic differences. It is in relation to this type of state, which is distinguished as such from that of 'Western democracy', that the difference between the exceptional regimes and the others should be measured, in the case of the dominated and dependent countries. In point of fact, even for those states that are not exceptional regimes, this type of dependent state has its particular features that distinguish it from analogous regimes in the dominant countries.

To come back to Portugal, Greece and Spain. All three of these have certain particular features in common. They are located, by their own internal structure, in the European arena, and yet they are still afflicted by a specific situation of dependence. The regimes that are replacing those of military dictatorship therefore present certain features of the dependent capitalist state, if to a lesser degree than is the case in other dominated countries. It is likely, therefore, that in view of the weakness of their bourgeoisies and their politico-ideological deficiencies, the state apparatuses in the strict (repressive) sense, and the armed forces in particular, will continue to play a specific and important ideological role, in parallel with the political parties. This is one of the features that seems to characterize the dependent state itself at the present time. It follows from this that the role of the military should not be seen, in the Greek or Spanish cases, for example, as a sign of the absence of any real break with the previous regimes (which would be the case if we had to compare these regimes with the 'Western democracies'). On the other hand, and this goes particularly for Portugal, the role of the armed forces, or a permanent institutionalization of the AFM, should neither be seen as in itself something out of the ordinary, possibly signifying a genuine and original road towards socialism. It could well be no more than the actual form that a bourgeois-'democratic' regime has to take in this country, even if in the event a progressive one.

Some of the lessons to be drawn from events in these countries apply also to other European countries, which are themselves dependent on the United States, if to a different degree. Although this is a different dependence, it gives rise to certain phenomena analogous to those that have been analysed here.

To take up again just one of these points, that of the present crisis of capitalism. This is a real structural crisis whose effects are very far from over, and in France and Italy in particular, it is directly leading to serious political crises. As is the case with every crisis of this kind, this threatens to put on the agenda the question of a possible rise of exceptional regimes, and the process leading up to this. In this context, might not the path followed in the countries we have been dealing with here to escape from the exceptional regimes indicate the path to be followed in other countries to prevent such regimes from arising? Once again here we must remind ourselves, as against the idyllic notion of certain people, that this path has its own inherent limitations, which have been indicated in this essay at a number of points. These involve the deep ambiguities associated with any process of alliance with fractions of the bourgeoisie, a process through which the domestic bourgeoisie most often succeeds in imposing its hegemony. They prove, if proof is needed, that it is far better to avoid having to take this route at all – better not to wait until the popular movement is on the defensive, when various kinds of 'historic compromise' appear as a possible recourse, *in extremis*, against an exceptional regime. Experience also shows that even if in certain particular cases, where exceptional regimes have been established for a long time, alliances of this kind may be concluded, these are however rarely possible in political crises preceding the installation of such regimes, when the bourgeoisie as a whole rapidly swings over to support a state of open war against the popular masses.

It is better, therefore, not to wait for this. In fact, these political crises may provide the chance for a process of transition to socialism and genuine national independence – particularly in France and Italy, on account of the place of these countries in the imperialist chain and the exceptional strength of the popular movement there. One condition for this, of course, is that this movement and its organizations do not simply wait in passive expectation of the 'great day', but work constantly to create such a moment.

If we confine ourselves to waiting, we will not get the 'great day' at all, but rather the tanks in the small hours of the morning.

February 1975

From March 1975 to June 1976

Every book has its date, and must be read with this in mind. But the importance of the events that have taken place in these countries since this book was first written makes some account of them essential. I have not attempted to revise the book itself, nor to provide a historical narrative of subsequent developments. I shall confine myself simply to the problems which these raise.

I. Portugal

My analysis stopped short just prior to Spinola's attempted coup of March 11th, 1975, and its defeat. But I had already based this on a fundamental thesis which, I believed, held good not simply for Portugal, but for Greece and Spain as well: the process of 'de-fascisization', or more properly the break with the military dictatorships, could not skip over a specific stage of democratization and be simply telescoped together with a transition to socialism. Of course, these are not stages separated by a Chinese wall, but rather the stages of an uninterrupted process. This thesis was based in turn on a whole series of analyses concerning the position of these countries in the imperialist chain, their class structure and class configuration, the lines of class alliance that were thereby drawn, the popular movement and its political organizations, as well as the particular paths by which the dictatorships were overthrown, etc. As far as Portugal in particular was concerned, while I drew attention to the characteristic instability of the democratization process, I predicted that it would probably follow an electoral road in the short or medium term.

The present situation in Portugal and the developments that occurred after the fall of Gonçalves – particularly after the left-wing military uprising of November 25th – certainly confirm this thesis. But the only reason I mention this is to raise the underlying question as to what exactly took place in Portugal between March 11th and November 25th, 1975. Was there really the beginning of a transition to socialism, as the overwhelming majority of observers thought at the time and continue to think now, a process whose failure was followed by a kind of reversion to the democratization stage after November 25th? Was it really impossible, as I maintained, to dispense with a specific stage of democratization, or were there in fact real possibilities of this that were not successfully exploited, essentially due to subjective 'error'? In the latter case, my thesis would have been verified *a posteriori*, but for different reasons than I had for putting it forward. This is an important question to answer, as the developments in Portugal between March 11th and November 25th assume a quite different significance according to the perspective adopted.

For my own part, I still believe we did not see the defeat of a transition to socialism that was already under way. At no point in the period in question did the Portuguese situation really break through the limits of the democratization stage. But this is not to say that there was not something at stake, and something lost, during these months. What exactly?

What is involved here is the question of the particular modalities of the democratization stage. In my analyses of Greece and Spain, I not only held that the democratization process could not be telescoped together with a transition to socialism, but also that this process was taking place (or would take place) under the hegemony of the domestic bourgeoisie – a fact that went together, as I saw it, with the absence of an anti-monopolist policy and alliance during this stage. The same was true of Portugal, I maintained, at the time I was writing, but in a much sharper fashion and with a marked instability. In the Portuguese case, I noted, there was the possibility in the near future of the democratization process taking place under the hegemony and leadership of the popular masses and their class organizations. The difference between a democratization stage and a transition to socialism, in fact, was not the only important question, and what was presently decisive was the question of the leadership of the democratization process itself, both from the economic aspect (anti-monopoly measures, etc.) and from the political aspect, too (the scope and tempo of the purging of state institutions and personnel handed down from the military dictatorship). What was really at stake in Portugal, then, and what was lost for a long while to come, was neither a transition to socialism (there was never a situation in which this was likely), nor the actual development of the democratization stage as such (there was no question of a return to fascism after November 25th, for example), but precisely the hegemony and leadership of this democratization process by the popular masses. This was won for a while under Gonçalves, as is attested to by a whole series of features that marked this historical acceleration, but it was later lost again, with the domestic bourgeoisie managing to reestablish its own hegemony.

There was not the beginning of a transition to socialism. I want to mention here a few major features of the period between March 11th and November 25th which confirm the analysis already given in the main part of the book.

1. Firstly, we have the level of consciousness and preparation of even that section of the popular masses that was most highly politicized and active during this period. It was certainly a period marked by a mobilization and radicalization of the section involved. Up to the eve of November 25th, Lisbon saw repeated demonstrations of a gigantic scale, often involving between two and five hundred thousand people, and with very advanced slogans. The experiments in 'popular power' also seemed to be making good progress, from factory

and community councils to the 'Soldiers United Will Win' movement. 'Red' military units such as RALIS, the Military Police and even some parachute regiments, were in open rebellion against the government in its capital, fraternizing with the masses, and so on.

What really happened on November 25th? To come straight to the point: a mere military picnic, which was hardly even a surprise for anyone. Jaime Neves' commandos, their loyalty ensured by the four fatal casualties they had sustained, seized the red bases and reestablished order with a wave of the hand, scarcely even firing a shot. A few of the most compromised soldiers and militants were arrested (this was the least that mattered), and even they were subsequently released. The operation was undoubtedly prepared for by the various measures taken by the Azevedo government after the fall of Gonçalves in September (in particular the demobilization of a large number of conscripts), but what matters most to us here, as an index of the consciousness of the most politicized masses in Portugal, is their attitude after November 25th. The important thing is *after* this event, for the fact that these masses were in no way involved in the vicissitudes of the ultra-left soldiers' uprising does not mean that they were not preparing for a transition to socialism. Now, after November 25th, and for more than two months, this radical mobilization simply vanished from one day to the next, at least at the most visible level, these masses being as it were barricaded at home or at their places of work, crushed, one might say, by the imaginary spectre of a return of the dictatorship. The first demonstration after these events, that organized by the Communist Party at the end of January, on the simple slogan of defending real wages, scarcely succeeded in attracting some ten to twenty thousand participants.

The point needs no argument on my part, for these are signs that cannot deceive, stubborn facts that cannot in any way be twisted. If even the most politicized and radicalized sections of the popular masses showed this attitude after November 25th, this already means that they were neither ready, *a fortiori*, for a transition to socialism, which would have required struggles of a far greater order. (The ultra-left soldiers' uprising, to repeat, does not come into question here.) Even if I am being somewhat schematic, the weight of this phenomenon speaks for itself, and cannot be explained in terms of the 'errors' made by organizations which did not prepare the masses – except by those for whom the masses are just a sacred cow. The real explanation must be sought elsewhere, in the fact that even the most politicized part of the Portuguese masses lacked the historical experience of open class struggle. This was the result of the long duration of the military dictatorship, so that the masses here did not even have traces of such struggle in their collective memory (a case quite different from those of Greece or Spain). Slowly and painfully, the Portuguese masses had to piece together their own experience of class struggle, starting from scratch. We can understand very well, therefore, how they sometimes believed that socialism would virtually be granted them by decree, and how they were not ready to fight to win it, but this in no way alters the situation, which is one of the objective coordinates that made any telescoping of the democratization stage with the transition to socialism impossible in Portugal.

2. The other coordinates have been sufficiently presented in the main body of the book, and I need only signal here the following.

a) During the period between March 11th and November 25th, the lines of class alliance were not really extended further. The radicalization of the popular masses in Portugal remained the radicalization of a minority, taking the country as a whole, and the campaigns of 'cultural dynamization' that the most left-wing elements of the Armed Forces Movement undertook were very far from producing the expected results. Even more: to the extent that the historical process accelerated, and in the face of certain forms that it sometimes assumed, a section of the popular masses who were already reserved in their attitude towards the radical alliance began to move towards open hostility. This was particularly the case with broad sections of the rural petty bourgeoisie in the North of the country, but it also affected the middle peasants in all areas. Major splits also became apparent within the class alliance that had existed when the dictatorship was overthrown. The domestic bourgeoisie fell away, and so did a significant section of higher and middle-level professional people, who fled the country on a massive scale, though this was not the most important factor, and was certainly to be expected in any case. Far more significant was the fact that sizeable fractions of the urban petty bourgeoisie came to detach themselves from the process that was under way (viz. among other things the rise of the PPD and the Socialist Party), while only an ever smaller minority of this petty bourgeoisie was being radicalized to the left.

But this was not all. Wider cracks began to appear within the working class itself. From July onwards, the Socialist Party showed a growing power to mobilize sections of the working class, while the divisions between socialist and communist workers became ever more acute – the vicissitudes of the Intersindical trade-union federation being only one aspect of this. No doubt the Socialist Party's anti-communist campaign, which fed on certain aspects of the Communist Party's policy, was largely responsible for this, but these divisions cannot be reduced to a struggle between organizations, with the masses simply tagging behind. If it is clear that those elements in the working class who followed the curious medley of actions undertaken by the Socialist Party were far from being generally more backward in relation to those who followed the Communist Party (in terms of less 'advanced' demands, for instance), there was still for all that a gap of some kind, along complex lines of division. Nor should we forget that the problems that arose led to many cases in which the working class went back on the experiments of self-management and popular power that were already set up, with the workers in some self-managed firms actually voting for the return of the former owners (under certain conditions). We must also add here the effect of the *retornados* from the African colonies; while these did not flock towards extreme right-wing movements as their French counterparts had to the OAS, their weight still acted as a brake on the revolutionary process.

b) Given Portugal's economic and social structure, and its place in the imperialist chain, the international context and the global balance of forces was bound to weigh heavily in the outcome. It need only be noted here that Portugal was only able to restrain, at least relatively, massive and direct foreign intervention, by two conditions that were respected right through this period. First, NATO bases and installations in Portugal were not to be touched. Secondly, nationalization was not to affect foreign capital, which, given the importance of this in the Portuguese economy, and the country's characteristic structure of dependence, already set firm limits to the Portuguese experiment.

Here too, however, we can clearly establish the fact that I noted earlier, i.e. that it was internal factors that played the principal role. The 'external' factors were not able to prevent the hegemony of the popular masses over the democratization process during this period, and did not play the principal role in their defeat. This is also to say that these 'external' factors only barred the way to a transition to socialism in Portugal in so far as they were articulated to the objective internal situation.

c) Despite first appearances, the organizational structure of the state apparatuses, or at least their hard core, showed a remarkable solidity, with the politicization of their agents exhibiting the limitations that I have stressed over the whole course of this period. It is true that, given the acceleration of the historic process after March 11th, we saw both a major purge in the agents of these apparatuses, and considerable changes in certain of the ideological apparatuses as well (newspapers, publishing, mass communication, education, etc.), even if these were not without their ambiguities. But on the one hand, the Church, as the dominant ideological apparatus, kept its influence almost intact, despite the confiscation of the Renascença radio station by the popular forces. While on the other hand the repressive apparatus, and the Army above all, kept its characteristically ambiguous position throughout the period in question, so that the contradictions within it that eventually broke out counted for much in the success of the November 25th operation.

It is already remarkable that the two main repressive pillars of the dictatorship, the National Republican Guard and the Public Security Police, not only had not been dismantled at the time I was writing (February 1975), but were not subsequently put in question either, remaining practically intact under the various Gonçalves governments. But to come to the armed forces proper, we now have firm proof that the AFM had only minority support in the officer corps all along, that it was riven throughout by major contradictions, and above all that the politicization of the majority of officers was ambiguous and had distinct limits. Not just the large section of 'professionalist' officers, but also a significant number of those actually enrolled in the AFM, were only committed to the revolutionary process on condition that the continuity of the state apparatus was maintained, and by way of the ideology of the army as pillar of public order and guarantor of national unity. Even after the purges that followed March 11th, the great majority of officers still sought to preserve hierarchical discipline and the unity of the armed forces. Reacting also to the 'Soldiers United Will Win' movement, most officers had distanced themselves from the acceleration of the revolutionary process before 25th November, as was well shown in the September elections for positions in the AFM, witnessing as these did a strong swing towards braking this process, if not an actual advance by the 'right'.

I am simply indicating these developments, but their significance is clear enough. The process in Portugal may well have been marked during this period by considerably heightened contradictions between the state apparatuses and their various branches, as well as within each of them, expressing among other things certain major dislocations within the state power, and the fact that the popular masses had won certain bastions. But the bourgeoisie's power was never dislodged, and it always had available its solid and practically unshaken seats in the hard core of these apparatuses. This situation was obscured by the shifting balance within these apparatuses, which contributed towards their inaction and temporary neutralization, but it was soon reestablished to the bourgeoisie's advantage.

What was the position, then, as far as the power and organization of the popular masses was concerned? I shall simply mention for the time being that while the masses did control some centres of power within the state apparatuses (COPCON, the 5th army division, as well as certain ideological apparatuses), and while there were therefore certain complex gaps between formal power and real power within these apparatuses, there was at no time the characteristic situation of dual power that results from the organization of a centralized popular power parallel and exterior to the official state apparatus, a major objective condition for a transition to socialism. Not only did the Intersindical federation become rapidly inoperative, as a function of its internal contradictions, but the various forms of popular power (workers' control, factory councils, commissions of *moradores* and peasant committees for agrarian reform, the soldiers' movements, etc.) basically remained in an embryonic and fragmentary state, lacking centralized coordination.

d) Finally, we must raise the question of the mass organizations. The first striking factor here is the absence of a mass revolutionary party with a consistent and well-adapted line for the transition to socialism in a European country such as Portugal, an essential condition for such a transition to take place. Certainly the Socialist Party could not make up for this absence, but neither could the Communist Party (I shall come back to this), to say nothing of the organizations of the extreme left.

One factor that must always be borne in mind here is the nature of the Armed Forces Movement, the preponderant force between 11th March and 25th November, as well as the precise role that the AFM played. The class representation role of the AFM, in fact, oscillated between the radicalized petty bourgeoisie and the conflictual alliance between a section of the petty bourgeoisie and the domestic bourgeoisie, rather than the AFM acting as organizer of the working class and the rural masses. The events of 1975 only confirmed this fact, despite the profound changes in the AFM's structure and policy during this period, among which we may list the character of its internal contradictions (from Carvalho to the Group of Nine), its political recantations (from the celebrated July document which called for the formation of organs of popular power, through to its vacillations before 25th November), the absence of organic ties with the popular masses (viz. the vicissitudes of 'cultural dynamization'), and finally its contradictory attitude towards the structure and role of the army itself (from military ultra-leftism to professionalism).

It is clear, for all that, that these transformations and the role played by the state apparatuses, the armed forces and the AFM, as well as by the political parties and organizations, can in no way be simply reduced to an analysis of their class functions. What the Portuguese experience has shown yet again, rather, is the relative autonomy of the political super-structure in relation to the various classes in struggle: a relative autonomy which I myself tended to neglect in this book. The political superstructure has shown signs of resist-ances, opacities and inertias of its own, of specific processes that have in no way always fitted neatly together with changes in the balance of forces in the class struggle, and the same can be said of relations between the struggles of organizations and their functions of class representation. The rise of the popular forces, in particular, is far from being directly reflected step by step, in a one to one fashion, within the state apparatuses. It is only by taking particular account of this relative autonomy, and therefore of the specific institu-tional framework of the state apparatuses, that we can under-stand what the Armed Forces Movement in Portugal has proved yet again, i.e. that an organization that has issued from the very heart of the bourgois military structure, and which thus follows the logic of this structure to a great extent, can in no case lead a process of transition to socialism.

The above remarks must at least suffice to show that there was no question of a transition to socialism in Portugal in the period in question; socialism was never really on the agenda. What did take place, however, was a shift in the leadership and the hegemony over the democratization process from the bourgeoisie to the popular masses. This was reflected in an acceleration of the democratization process for certain of the state apparatuses, in major nationalization measures that affected big monopoly capital (some 50 per cent of all capital was nationalized), in agrarian reform in the South of the country, in a significant improvement in the standard of living of the popular masses, in the increased weight of the workers in their places of work, in the establishment of embryonic organizations of a 'workers' control' type, etc. But what I would like to dwell on for a moment here are the reasons that led to the defeat of this hegemony of the working class and popular masses over the democratization process.

1. Some of these reasons are the same as those already mentioned with regard to the actual impossibility, in Portugal, of the democratization stage being telescoped together with a stage of transition to socialism: more specifically, the absence of powerful and massively implanted class organizations (unions, left-wing parties) able to coordinate and unify the masses' initiatives, and in particular the absence of a mass revolutionary party, whose role, we must underline yet again, proves indispensable not only for the 'socialist revolution', but also for the hegemony of the popular classes in a process of democratization. The striking thing in Portugal, in fact, more so than the 'errors' of one organization or other, is the chaotic, fragmentary and contradictory character of popular initiatives, and of initiatives taken by the various organizations, with a complete absence of any real coordination. Abundant examples of this can be given, such as the strike movement, the popular power attempts, land occupations, take-overs of unoccupied houses, self-management experiments, measures concerning the ideological apparatuses as well as movements

within the armed forces.

The second reason for this defeat was the absence of an alliance between the organizations of the left on a democratization programme with clearly defined objectives. A popular unity of this kind at the organizational level was sadly lacking in Portugal. It is true that these organizations rallied to the draft programme of the AFM before the April 1975 elections, but this programme was pretty vague. Subsequent events showed that for all the parties concerned, each with their different reasons, this was a purely formal and superficial unity, all the more so in that this programme was far from expressing any unified position on the part of the AFM itself, this organization being in a constant state of flux, and riven throughout by deep contradictions. In this respect the period in question displays a real ballet of successive establishments and breakdowns of organizational and conjunctural understandings, from the fluctuating relations between the Socialist and Communist Parties to the more heteroclite ties that united the Socialists and the MRPP (Maoist organization), or the Communists and the front of far-left organizations. The game is complicated still further when we take account of the relations between these organizations on the one hand, and the various fractions of the AFM (COPCON, the 5th division, the 'moderate' sectors, etc.) and the armed forces as a whole on the other hand. From a certain point onwards, these relations are at least as much a product of struggles for influence on the political stage, and the purely organizational relationships that this involves, as anything corresponding to the real relationships of class struggle. These factors not only prevented the coordination and unification of the mass movement, but in fact actually contributed to its division and disorientation.

2. We must now deal with the attitude of the major left-wing organizations and their concrete policies, both as regards the characterization of the stage in general, and as regards the process taking place and the real balance of forces involved.

a) The Socialist Party. This party only confirmed its social-democratic character, and the basically rightist orientation of its leadership. Its policy was never more than that of a democratization process under the hegemony of the domestic bourgeoisie, and as the process accelerated, it progressively showed itself a privileged representative of this class. If it rallied to the anti-monopoly measures taken by the Gonçalves governments, this was only in self-defence, and under pressure from its base. It sought throughout to restrain the process and leant irresistibly towards the PPD, while always keeping open a certain terrain of compromise with foreign capital and with the monopolist and comprador big bourgeoisie. Its passionate anti-communism, fed as this was by the PCP's own policy and errors, conveniently enabled it to present itself as the champion of democratization, as against the unrealistic character of certain aspects of PCP policy. With the PCP tending to telescope together the process of democratization and the transition to socialism, and given the model of socialism and the ways of attaining it that the PCP had adopted, the Socialist Party was able to use its democratic cover to conceal the real alternative that it represented – not merely a realistic process of democratization as against an unrealistic transition to socialism, but rather a process of democratization under bourgeois leadership and hegemony. On the other hand, however, it is equally clear that the Socialist Party did not itself represent the 'reaction' of the comprador bourgeoisie or the big landowners, and the assimilation of Soares to Spinola which would seek to give this impression serves no function other than that of abuse.

b) The Communist Party. The first thing to note here, in so far as Western opinion has had all too great a tendency to charge the PCP with all the alleged 'sins' of the Portuguese experiment, is that this party played only a relatively limited role, as regards both its social weight and its political initiatives. It was far from having the dominant role in the period which concerns us here, nor in a whole series of affairs, such as that of the *Republica* newspaper for example, that were immediately charged to its account.

That being said, the fact remains that the party's policy, in as much as it was actually effective, was frequently characterized not only by an under-estimate of the balance of forces, but also and particularly by an almost systematic oscillation between orientation to a democratization stage and to a stage of transition to socialism – by a remarkable confusion, in fact. Its policy was one of constant fluctuations, of advances and retreats, of acceleration and brake, with perpetual zigzags: support for strike movements that really were untimely, followed by restraint on strikes or even their denunciation; support for the most radical forms of popular power ('Soldiers United Will Win', for instance), coupled with the rejection of any centralized organization; tailing behind certain ultra-left sections of the AFM (particularly after the dismissal of Gonçalves from office in September), while taking its distance from COPCON and Carvalho at crucial moments; failure to struggle against the repressive institutions bequeathed by the dictatorship (the National Republican Guard and the Public Security Police), while using the 5th army division which it controlled to try and take over the AFM; a policy of unity with the Socialists, with the PCP permanently in the government, but combined with an ultra-left tactic towards the Socialists reminiscent of the Comintern's notorious Third Period (1928–34), almost treating the Socialist Party as social-fascist; accepting limitations to the agrarian reform while unconditionally supporting 'wildcat' occupations of land. The list is a long one and I shall not rub it in, as the PCP has already made its own self-criticism. But what I would like to draw attention to, in any case, is that it would be wrong to view this policy of the PCP's as a consistent whole, marked in its entirety by ultra-left features. It is far more accurate to see this as a deeply contradictory policy, made up of successive advances and retreats with effects that are rightist and ultra-left at the same time: rightist in the context of the PCP's anticipated transition to socialism, and ultra-left in its perspective of a democratization stage. These two opposed perspectives actually coexisted throughout in the policy of the Portuguese Communist Party.

But this is only one aspect of the problem, and in the last analysis the least important. The decisive aspect involves the PCP's vision and practical attitude as regards the road to socialism and the seizure of power by the popular masses. I say 'decisive' not just because the question of socialism was permanently on the agenda after 11th March 1975, as far as the PCP was concerned, alongside the question of the democratization process, but also because its vision and its practical attitudes as regards the road to socialism quite clearly governed its policy as regards the democratization process itself.

This is undoubtedly a very broad problem. It involves such important questions as the choice between a minoritarian and vanguardist development towards socialism or a process based on the active support of the broad popular masses, a strategy for the conquest of power by frontal attack and a war of movement or a protracted process of positional warfare (these two pairs of alternatives do not precisely overlap), as well as the question of civil liberty and democracy during the transition and under the socialist regime, etc. But although these questions are all bound up together, I want to confine myself more specifically to that of the attitude of the PCP towards the state and the capture of political power, for it is probably this which most heavily marked its practice during the democratization process.

This question is all the more complex in that it cannot be confined, as many people seek to do, to a simple strategic alternative, i.e. either a frontal, insurrectionary and precisely located attack like the assault on the Winter Palace, which the PCP is alleged to have followed, or a protracted process of positional warfare which the PCP allegedly ignored. A party's attitude towards the state goes well beyond this alternative, and a false conception here, such as that of the PCP, can appear equally in one strategy or the other, for it is in no way self-evident that the PCP followed this former strategy, though its false position on the question of the state marked its entire policy from beginning to end.

The decisive problem, in fact, as far as a democratization process under the leadership of the popular masses was concerned, was that the masses had to win solid bases for their own political power. This problem has two facets to it: a) to organize forms of popular power parallel to the state apparatuses proper (I shall come back to this); b) to conquer bases of power actually within the state apparatuses. What was the practice of the PCP in this respect? Fundamentally, we can say, its policy was a narrowly partisan one, in the sense of seeking to consolidate an 'organizational' influence based largely on an almost conspiratorial infiltration and on installing 'trustworthy people' in key positions; a policy, therefore, that was technicist and bureaucratic, centering on the organization of branches and apparatuses that it tightly controlled, and which it could use to take over and short-circuit the state 'machine' (the 5th division affair among others). Such a policy goes together with the instrumentalist conception of the state that I explained in the main body of the book, the conception of the state as a 'tool' or 'machine' whose conquest is seen, in the last analysis, in terms of 'manipulation' by one's agents, and the colonization of its component cogs. This is undoubtedly one of the reasons that led the PCP to stick so closely to the policy of the AFM, embracing all the latter's vicissitudes for the sake of winning control of the AFM through the 5th division. This whole conception ignores the fact that the state is the material condensation of a balance of class forces, as this balance is expressed within it in a specific way, and therefore that the class struggle runs right through the state itself. By failing to take account of this, the instrumentalist conception of the state leads to a politics unable to pose the question of struggle within the state apparatuses in the process of the conquest of power in terms of mass struggle and class alliance, and sees this question simply in terms of the seizure of the state-machine by an organization (the party). This is the indisputable root of a whole series of errors made by the PCP, to which were added, here too, those deriving from its under-estimation of the balance of forces and its confusion between the democratization stage and the transition to socialism.

c) The AFM. This is all the more important in so far as it was the AFM that played the dominant role throughout the period in question, certain aspects of this having already been mentioned. Given the absence of a mass revolutionary party, the dominant role of this organization, directly issuing from the institutional framework of the bourgeois state, contributed in the long run towards preventing the pursuance of the democratization process under the hegemony of the popular masses, even though the AFM was an essential component of the popular masses and would have been able to provide a decisive support for this hegemony. It could not, however, continue to be the driving motor. For a process of democratization which was under the hegemony of the popular masses, the limitations involved in the leading role of an AFM that was permanently torn between those sectors imbued with military ultra-leftism who considered themselves involved in a transition to socialism (an ultra-leftism that culminated in the insurrectionary movement of 25th November), and other sectors leaning towards bourgeois hegemony over the democratization process, marked the whole period between 11th March and 25th November, and were very clear just before that latter date. It was particularly apparent after the fall of Gonçalves in September that the hegemony of the popular masses over the democratization process (even a renegotiated hegemony) could only continue on the basis of a compromise between Carvalho's COPCON and the Group of Nine: a compromise which failed on the eve of 25th November owing to the ultra-left attitude of certain COPCON sectors (as Carvalho himself put it), though also to the very nature of the AFM.

d) The far left organizations. These showed such diversity in Portugal that it is impossible to deal with them in any general way. What should be noted is the significant role of the extreme left in comparison with other European countries, combined with the overwhelming predominance of 'Maoist' or 'pro-Chinese' groups, the MRPP at their head. As far as these latter are concerned, and their politics can be very sharply distinguished from those of other far-left organizations, the evidence is convincing: by treating the PCP, seen as 'social-fascist', as the main enemy, by transplanting into Portugal a Chinese foreign policy which views the USSR as the main enemy and leads in practice to preferring American hegemony and the right-wing forces in Europe, by the basic support that they gave the leadership of the Socialist Party, all this being combined with ultra-left demagogy, these groups incontestably bear a considerable share of responsibility for the failure of the Portuguese experiment.

3. These elements taken together explain the deeply contradictory character of the general policy followed in Portugal during the period in question, a permanent policy of either too much or too little, which subjected the alliance of the popular classes to severe strains, and led to the failure of their leadership over the democratization process. What I particularly want to draw attention to here, however, is the general lesson that may be drawn as regards the question of the state in a process of this kind, a lesson which is of the highest importance for all of us.

On the one hand, if the popular masses wish to win the leadership of the process for themselves, and therefore their own bases of political power, they must organize without fail forms of popular power at the base (workers' control, community and factory councils, peasant committees, etc.), outside and parallel to the state apparatuses proper. This struggle for the conquest of power bases can never be reduced to a struggle simply within the state apparatuses, even at the stage of democratization. These embryos of popular power and the self-organization of the masses played a decisive role in Portugal as far as establishing the hegemony of the popular masses over the democratization process was concerned.

On the other hand, however, and particularly in so far as there is no immediate transition to socialism, these forms of popular power cannot be organized in a central coordinating instance of a dual power type (the soviet model). This cannot be done by way of the left-wing parties or unions involved in this popular power; still less can it be done 'spontaneously'.

The reason that the left failed in Portugal is not because it did not attempt this operation, which was actually impossible in the objective circumstances of a democratization process. The reason must be sought elsewhere; to the extent that these forms of power, while they are indispensable if the leadership of the process is to devolve on the popular masses, cannot assume at this stage a centralized organizational structure, and develop the framework of a parallel state, they must of necessity depend on the existing state apparatus itself. This in turn evidently means two things.

a) The state apparatus within which the popular masses are to win themselves bastions of power must itself be profoundly transformed (democratized) in its structure, this being already a condition for a democratization process under the hegemony of the popular masses, and having also been attempted in practice by the Portuguese left.

b) This state apparatus besieged by the popular masses must however be able to continue to function as an operational unity. Not only can there be no question of 'smashing' it at this stage, but its 'democratization' must not involve its dismantling. This is actually shown by the Portuguese experience. In the context of a democratization stage in which the popular masses and their organizations have succeeded in besieging the state apparatus in a major way, to dismantle, disarticulate or split this apparatus under the vague pretext that the state should 'wither away' in favour of a 'popular power' that can as yet be no more than embryonic (this 'withering away' would in fact assume that the socialist revolution had already been accomplished), is the best way of enabling the bourgeoisie to reconquer those positions that the masses have obtained in the state. The dismantling and carving-up of the Portuguese state apparatus in the period we are dealing with, which was due both to the divisions of the left and to the ultra-left, enabled the bourgeoisie to maintain firm and unshaken bastions for itself, upset the effective neutralization of these bastions, and perhaps most important, prevented the left from obtaining state support for the new forms based on popular power (agricultural cooperatives, firms under self-management), when these came under attack from the right. There are innumerable cases of experiences of this kind which were supported by a large section of the left, but which came to grief for lack of the state action and support that the masses demanded. These cases are particularly significant in so far as the majority of them in no way involved a 'boycott' by state apparatuses or personnel; the problem was rather one of apparatuses that had been besieged by the masses, and bastions of their power, which were however condemned to inactivity in the general context of a disarticulation of the state apparatuses.

These were the fundamental reasons for the defeat of the democratization process in Portugal under the leadership of the popular masses. The elections of April 1975, on the other hand, although they played a part by the legitimacy that they brought the Socialist Party, had only a limited role in this defeat, contrary to a whole series of analyses (including those of the PCP) that tended to see the organization of these elections as the basic 'error' that was committed. For a country like Portugal, in fact, the democratization process could not but involve elections sooner or later. But if these other factors had been different, it is unlikely that the elections, whose function had in fact been already fixed in advance by the agreement between the political parties and the AFM, and whose result was very far from favourable to the right (the Socialist Party, the PCP and the MDP together winning more than 54 per cent of the votes), would have put in question the leadership of the popular masses in the democratization process. These elections, in fact, only had their effects *a posteriori*, i.e. once the balance of forces had already shifted in favour of the bourgeoisie.

The leadership and hegemony of the popular masses in the democratization process during this particular period was reflected in an accelerated democratization of certain apparatuses, and in important measures that I have already mentioned, such as nationalizations, agrarian reform in the South, etc. These measures cannot be judged as socialist or not in the abstract, except in those cases with advanced forms of workers' control: but they could have amounted to an initial instalment of socialist measures in the context and perspective of a stage of transition to socialism. In actual fact, progressive as they are, these measures, situated in the context of a process of democratization, have not in themselves broken the framework of bourgeois relations, and this is how they function as of now, given that the perspective of a socialist transition is no longer close. Despite the wage freeze policy, none of these measures was basically challenged after the 25th November, the popular masses having essentially succeeded in retaining their gains, at least up till now. This itself shows that these measures (nationalizations and agrarian reform) do not in themselves challenge the capitalist system and the power of the bourgeoisie. The balance of forces has certainly changed, and so it would be surprising if the near future did not see a certain reversal; however the bourgeoisie does not need to eliminate these gains in order to keep itself in power, as some people believed when, brought up on the comforting illusions of the intrinsically socialist character of these measures, they anticipated their radical elimination after 25th November.

All this will of course depend on the further evolution of the balance of class forces. And if the original lines of the popular class alliance were not extended in the period leading up to 25th November, nor this alliance solidified, even if fractions of these classes took their distance, as we saw, from the accelerated course that the democratization process then followed, it remains none the less true that this popular alliance was not basically broken in the face of the defection of the domestic bourgeoisie: these fractions of the people did not swing over to the side of reaction, contrary to what was happening in Chile, for example, even before the fall of Allende. The alliance of popular classes, despite its vicissitudes and its cracks, despite even the divisions of the left-wing organizations, is still holding up. Moreover, if 25th

November was certainly a reversal, it was not a crushing defeat for the working class and the popular masses, who had carefully avoided involvement in the military left's adventure of an uprising. This also explains how it was that 25th November did not see the aggressive return of 'reaction' in the form of the big landowners and comprador bourgeoisie. Not just in the sense that the forces of reaction failed to make such a comeback, but also in that 25th November never had this class meaning from the start, as against those fantastic conceptions that see behind Antunes and Eanes the shadow of fascism, just as similar fantasies saw socialism on the agenda before 25th November. To put it schematically, while 25th November certainly restored the hegemony of the domestic bourgeoisie over the democratization process, it also reconstituted the alliance of the popular classes (the PCP in particular has kept its place in the government) in the context of a change in the balance of forces and the inability of the popular forces to maintain their leadership of the process. 25th November did not put the democratization process in question, even if certain safety catches against a return of 'reaction' were necessarily sprung. I am even tempted to say that, given how the Portuguese experiment was developing, 25th November was the least evil that could have happened; for unless we want to delude ourselves completely and rebuild history on the basis of 'if's', we have to admit that Portugal was heading at break-neck speed towards catastrophe. The popular masses, to be sure, still have arrears to pay for this reestablishment of bourgeois hegemony, but the future is fundamentally preserved, even if this future may now have to be seen as a distant one, the democratization process having been incontestably stabilized in favour of the bourgeoisie.

II. Spain

As it was Portugal that presented most in the way of new problems after this book was first published, I can be more brief on the subjects of Spain and Greece.

The development that has taken place in Spain confirms that regimes of military dictatorship are incapable of reforming themselves, i.e. of exhibiting a continuous and linear internal evolution towards a form of 'parliamentary-democratic' regime that would replace its predecessor by way of an ordered 'succession'. It shows that the democratization process can not get going without a democratic 'break' with the institutional framework of the previous regime.

This break has not yet taken place in Spain, despite the significant changes on the political stage after the death of Franco. This political stage must never be confused with the organizational structure of the state apparatuses, and in the Spanish case this structure remains as yet fundamentally unchanged. 'Fundamentally', for the necessity of a break bears on the transition to a 'parliamentary-democratic' type of state, and does not mean that in the absence of this break and the associated transition, these dictatorships are condemned to pure immobility. Depending on the conjuncture, they can permit certain internal changes, but these are narrowly restricted in their specific context. This is what has happened in Spain, where the changes so far signify above all a redisposition of forces in view of impending struggles. Fraga's 'reforming' velleities of a 'continuist' and controlled transition towards a healthy democracy, for instance, seem unable to stand the test of a rise in popular struggles, which lead the 'reforming' wing of the regime to lean irresistibly for support on the 'bunker' and the 'immobilists' (viz. the massive and bloody repression that struck Spain in February–March 1976). The main contradiction as far as the transformation of the regime is concerned is not that between the 'bunker' and the reforming tendency, but rather between the latter and the forces committed to a break.

As far as this process of a democratic break is concerned, I simply want to note the following points:

1. Its beginning is somewhat tardy, compared to what one might have thought before the death of Franco. And there

are three basic reasons for this.

First, the extreme franquista right wing has shown that it still enjoys an undeniable popular support, something that I underestimate in this book in holding that the support that Franco had managed to win had practically disappeared, and that the organizations of the ultra-right were now only ossified relics. In fact, both the Ex-Combatants Association and the various Falangist groupings have shown a surprising vitality.

Secondly, there is the question of the present political positions of the domestic bourgeoisie. Given its internal contradictions and the political and ideological limitations that I already stressed, a significant section of this bourgeoisie which was swinging towards the *Plataforma de Convergencia* and the *Junta Democratica* when attempts at democratization failed under Franco, seems at the moment, now that Franco is dead, to have set its sights instead on Fraga's 'reformist' way out of the franquista regime (even though this is in fact a blind alley). Once again they believe they can have their cake and eat it too, transform the regime without having to undergo the risks involved and pay the necessary price.

Finally, a third reason. It bears once again on the relative autonomy of the franquista state vis-à-vis the classes in struggle, and particularly vis-à-vis the power bloc. Here too I tended to under-estimate this, as I did in the case of my Portuguese analysis. This relative autonomy is very clear in the resistance and inertia that the franquista state exhibits, often despite the reformist velleities of certain sectors of the government, and also despite the political positions of a large wing of the power bloc. It is only in this way that one can understand the considerable institutional weight that the 'bunker' still enjoys within the state apparatus. The same relative autonomy can be seen in the specific paths taken by internal contradictions within the state apparatus, particularly within the army. Here these contradictions persist and intensify (formation of the Military Democratic Union), but they are none the less contained by, or rather channelled into, the specific circuits and networks of the franquista apparatus.

Taken together, these elements still leave open several opportunities for the ultra-right and the hard core of these apparatuses to launch a preventive intervention designed to forestall the impending liquidation of the regime.

2. The strength of the popular movement and the left-wing organizations, with the Spanish Communist Party at their head, has been amply confirmed. The prospect before us is still one in which, given the absence in the Spanish case of anything like the Portuguese colonial wars or the Cyprus affair for Greece, it will be the development of this popular movement, articulated to the internal contradictions of the state apparatus, that will directly form the determinant element unleashing the democratic break, whatever might be the forms that this process takes. One fact of fundamental importance here is certainly that of the progressively cemented unity of the left-wing and democratic organizations (the fusion of the *Plataforma de Convergencia* and the *Junta Democratica* in March 1976), in the face of the government's attempt to divide these forces, and particularly to isolate the Communist Party. This unity is largely due to the policy followed by the Spanish Communist Party, which is quite distinct from that of its Portuguese counterpart.

These notes do not seek to foreclose the concrete forms that the democratization process might assume. The separation between the political and governmental stage and the organizational structure of the apparatuses, to which we have already drawn attention, could possibly work two ways. If the changes that have taken place on the political stage after Franco's death have in no way corresponded to a democratic break within the state apparatuses, it can still not be ruled out that a genuine break might get under way, at least for a time, with a section of the political and governmental personnel still unchanged (viz. for example the recent proposal by the Communist Party for a government of national unity). This will also depend on the path taken by the internal contradictions on this stage and among these personnel.

III. Greece

I shall deal equally briefly with Greece, which presents a process of relatively stable democratization under the hegemony and direction of the domestic bourgeoisie. The democratization process has continued without any real reversal, so that Greece is now living under a 'parliamentary-democratic' regime such as has been practically unknown since 1936 (when the Metaxas dictatorship was established). The state personnel handed down by the dictatorship have been to a substantial extent purged (the armed forces, police, gendarmerie), and their main leaders tried and condemned to long terms of imprisonment. This would seem to exclude a new rise of reaction, at least in the short run. The division between the liberal right and the ultra-right has persisted, this expressing the relative autonomy of the political instance, of the internal contradictions of the power bloc, as always with its specific phasing.

The Greek case, however, also confirms how a democratization process of this kind has very distinct limits. These limits are, in essentials, not something specific to Greece, but rather a product of more general factors. They bear in fact on the developing crisis of hegemony that is now affecting all the Western bourgeoisies, and which is giving rise in all these countries, to a varying degree, to a new form of bourgeois state with certain specific characteristics of the 'strong' or 'authoritarian' state. Certain aspects of the Greek developments, in fact, are simply the counterpart of what is taking place in France or Germany. In Greece, however, these limits are also related to the particular features of the domestic bourgeoisie, in the context of a process of democratization under its hegemony. These involve a terrain of compromise with the comprador bourgeoisie and foreign capital, which has been renegotiated but is permanently open; a contradictory policy vis-à-vis the Atlantic Alliance (a tendency towards military reintegration with NATO, combined with restriction on the privileges of American bases); a hesitant and fluctuating policy as regards the democratization of the state apparatuses and the purging of their personnel, the tendency being to maintain certain forces bequeathed by the dictatorship in case things turn really bad for the bourgeoisie; attempts to tie the hands of the workers' and popular movement (anti-strike measures for example), and to check the gains this has made, while keeping the terrain of compromise open.

The form taken by the democratization process in Greece also relates to the situation of the popular movements and popular struggles. Two characteristic features must be mentioned here.

a) The movement has exhibited a considerable degree of development, politicization and combativeness (imposing measures of democratization on the bourgeoisie), but this is not reflected at the level of the opposition organizations, and particularly the organizations of the left, which still remain relatively weak. This in turn restricts the popular movement itself. What is involved here is in fact a crisis of representation between the popular movement and its own organizations. Among other things, this crisis is a product of the repeated errors of these organizations, and particularly of the Greek Communist Party, on the establishment of the Metaxas dictatorship (1936), at the culmination of the Resistance struggles (particularly the failure of the Athens insurrection in late 1944), during the Civil War (1946–49), and finally, at the time that the colonels seized power in 1967. Four successive and bloody defeats are probably too much for entire generations of militants.

b) This crisis of representation which limits the impact of the popular movement is also related to the nature of some of the left-wing organizations as such, and the deep divisions among them – a factor that has proved persistent, and is becoming yet sharper. To take the socialist organizations first of all. For a whole series of reasons, there has never been a significant socialist or social-democratic party in Greece. Andreas Papandreou's PASOK is no exception to this; it is rather a populist movement that has been radicalized to the left, and is basically oriented to the urban and rural petty bourgeoisie (this latter being still important in Greece). PASOK is organized around the 'charismatic' personality of its leader, and it exhibits all the classical signs of populism: in particular, it is opposed to any alliance of left-wing organizations under the pretext of 'keeping its hands free' and first strengthening its own influence.

The most important question, however, is the position of the Greek Communist Party, and particularly the significance of its 1968 split into the 'Interior' and 'Exterior' parties. This situation is particularly badly known in France, due among other things to the silence of the PCF, which, contrary to the practice of the Spanish, Italian, Yugoslav, British and Swedish CPs, only recognizes the 'party of the Exterior'. We can say rather schematically that the Greek Communist Party, as a function of its recent experience in the Civil War and the characteristic intervention of the Soviet Union in its affairs, became the focus of the contradictions between the European communist movement and the USSR, with the Soviets succeeding in splitting the Greek party in the way that Carillo prevented them from doing with the Spanish party (the Lister affair). The Greek Communist Party 'of the Interior' (so-called because it arose from the majority of the central committee, and almost all members of the committee who were situated in Greece under the dictatorship – against the minority based in the Eastern countries) is the more important, both from an organizational viewpoint and by virtue of the considerable influence and audience that it enjoys. Its development prefigured the path of independence from the USSR that has since been followed by several other European parties. At the present time it follows a line of 'anti-fascist alliance', deeming that the crucial problem in Greece, in the present conjuncture, is still the deepening and acceleration of the democratization process. Its policy therefore consists firstly in an alliance between the forces of the left, secondly between these forces and the democratic opposition, though taking account also of the contradictions in the enemy camp (right and ultra-right).

The Communist Party 'of the Exterior', for its part, is the

last of the West European parties to retain its 'Stalinist' features. Its practice could be described as a kind of Cunhalism without the masses, this party being relatively weak and isolated. One must also note its total organizational and political dependence on the USSR, a dependence that actually takes the form of caricature; the greater part of its energies, moreover, are spent in fighting the Communist Party 'of the Interior'.

This division among the forces of the left thus limits the impact of popular struggles, and has contributed to a stabilization of bourgeois hegemony over the democratization process.

Index

Printed by Printforce, United Kingdom